"HISTOR[illegible] Y
OF LIN[illegible]
COMMEN[illegible] ROFESSOR
M. R. SAKHARE'S BOOK

A Critical Review

Fifth Edition

LINGA RAJU, M. D.

"History and Philosophy of Lingayat Religion"
Commentary on Professor M. R. Sakhare's
Book
A Critical Review

Fifth Edition

This fifth edition soft cover print book has been slightly modified from the original fifth edition book with the same ISBN 9781521090886.

Linga Raju, M. D.

Modified August 2024

Table of Contents

Introduction

The book on which this commentary is written is titled 'HISTORY AND PHILOSOPHY OF LINGĀYAT RELIGION.' by M. R. Sakhare, M. A., T. D. (Cantab), published by the Karnataka University, Dharwad, India, in the year 1978 (1).

Professor M. R. Sakhare's book has been referenced to by me in many of my articles and books. Indeed, this scholarly work in English has been referred to in the past by students of Philosophy and Religion to better understand the Religious Philosophy of Lingāyatas who are also known as Veerashaivas.

Although Professor Sakhare's book has been regarded as one of the authentic works in English on this subject, some questions have been raised on some parts of the book and on some of his opinions. Therefore, Professor Sakhare's book was reviewed, and then, as it seemed appropriate to report the findings, this commentary was submitted to the interested and concerned readers.

It is said in Professor Sakhare's book, that the Veerashaiva philosophy and practices have a distinct place in the religious history of India, but this had not been realized by many scholars including the western scholars because much of the literature on the subject was in Kannada language and not fully published in Sanskrit. Professor Sakhare had published a book, in the year 1942, translating the Sanskrit 'Lingadharanachandrika' into English. Professor Sakhare's original book had included 'History and Philosophy of Lingayat Religion' as an introduction to the textual part of Lingadharanachandrika and its translation and notes.

The Karnataka University thought that the then available Veerashaiva literature in English was inadequate to meet the demands of the public and the students of Philosophy and Religion. Therefore, the University thought of reprinting some of the authentic works in English on the subject to meet the demands. By then, Professor Sakhare had already attained Lingaikya (had died), therefore, the University obtained permission from the family and from the Literary Committee of the L. E. Association, Dharwad, to reprint only the Introductory part of the original book, leaving out all the other parts. The book was then published in the year 1978.

The book has 'Foreword' reprinted from the 1942 First Edition, written by Dr. S. Radhakrishnan, 'Preface' written by the Vice-Chancellor of Karnataka University, 'Argument' written by the author, and fifteen chapters.

Professor Sakhare's Original Book

Professor Sakhare's original book, published in the year 1942, was an English translation of 'Lingadharanachandrika' which had been composed in Sanskrit by Shrī Nandikeshvara in the seventeenth century of the Common Era (CE/AD). The Lingadharanachandrika had been printed and published at Benares by the Swami of Kashimath (Jangamvadi of Benares), a pontifical seat of Vishvaradhya, one of the five Veerashaiva Acharyas. Professor Sakhare's original book had included 'History and Philosophy of Lingayat Religion' as an introduction to Lingadharanachandrika, as well as the textual part of Lingadharanachandrika, and the translation and the notes.

The Foreword for this original book had been written by Dr. S. Radhakrishnan. He was one of the scholars who wrote on the history of Indian Philosophy. He was a strong advocate of the Vedantic Advaita Philosophy, a slightly modified Advaita Philosophy of Shankaracharya. Doctor S. Radhakrishnan, later, after India's attainment of independence from the British, became the first Vice-

President of Independent India and then the second President of India. Some of what he wrote in the foreword for the original book is as follows.

'There is an increasing interest, both in India and abroad, in the works on Indian thought. While there were scholarly works in English on many branches of Indian Philosophy and Religion, there is no significant exposition of the Lingayat system by learned scholars. The world of scholars will welcome the publication of this important work on the Lingayat Religion by Professor Sakhare. The author takes great pains to make out that the Lingayat faith is altogether independent of the Hindu Religion. I am afraid that this is taking a somewhat narrow view of the spirit of Hinduism.'

The Author Professor Sakhare

The Late Professor M. R. Sakhare, M. A., T. D. (Cantab) was a Sanskrit Professor at the Lingaraj College in Belgaum, Karnataka State, India. He was one of the founding members of the K. L. E. society. In addition to his enormous work in the field of Education in developing the G. A. High School, Lingaraj College and other Institutions started by the K. L. E. society, he has done great scholarly work.

Professor Sakhare, at the beginning of the book, under 'Argument', states that he had long cherished a desire to place before the reading world the Philosophy and principles of the Lingayat religion. The main reason for that desire, the Professor says, was that Lingāyatism was not much known outside Karnataka, that even in Karnataka it was known as kind of Shaivism with another alternative name of Veerashaivism, and that the Lingāyatas were said to be a Shaiva sect wearing Linga on their bodies and being outside the sphere of Brahminic influence.

Further, Professor Sakhare states that, Lingāyatas themselves do not know what their religion is and what its history is, much less others. To dissipate the wrong ideas and to place before the reading and the thoughtful public the facts of the religion was his long-cherished desire. And after his return from England, the Professor says, he began to seriously think of undertaking the heavy responsibility and the enormous and onerous task of setting forth and explaining the principles of the religion. He states that, because Linga worn on the body is not only the most prominent characteristic of the religion but also its basis and central point, he has made 'Lingadharanachandrika' to be the basis of his thesis and has presented his work.

Professor Sakhare then makes this following statement on page xii under 'Argument': "*Though I am positively of the opinion that Vachana Shastra is the basic literature of the religion as its scriptures, I have based all my thesis with profuse quotations on Sanskrit books for the simple reason that my thesis centers round a Sanskrit work*".

Right at the outset the readers should make note of this - most of what Professor Sakhare says in his book is not taken from the main scripture of the Lingāyatas. Professor Sakhare's original book was published in the year 1942.

Veerashaiva and Lingāyata

The first chapter in this book is titled 'Veerashaiva and Lingayata'. Professor Sakhare starts with the statement that 'Lingadharanachandrika is a treatise written to establish the principle and creed of wearing Linga on the body by the Veerashaivas or Lingayatas', and then he continues his discussion on the terms Veerashaiva and Lingayata.

The term 'Veerashaiva' has been etymologically defined and elaborately explained in treatises and literature of the religion. The term 'Veerashaivism' is of the same age as that of the origin of that religion itself, whenever that might be. But the origin of the word 'Lingayata' is not only obscure but also conspicuously absent in religious literature and is neither defined nor explained therein. The term 'Lingayata' is comparatively a later one to have come into vogue, and it prominently expresses the followers of Veerashaivism, and signifies unmistakably those who wear on their bodies the holy Linga. The word 'Veerashaiva' does not bring out the idea of Linga worn on the body as strikingly as the word 'Lingayata' does. The term 'Veerashaiva' is less common in ordinary language, but the term 'Lingayata' is ordinarily more common and more known. That is why, Professor Sakhare says, the term 'Lingayata' is used in the title of the book.

Professor Sakhare, then, gives his opinion and explanation of the origin of the word 'Lingayata'. He believes that it is derived from the Sanskrit compound word *'Lingavat'* which means 'one who possesses Linga'; the word *'Lingavantah',* being the nominative plural, applies to many individuals who possess Linga. The two Sanskrit words, the Professor says, must have been first used by the educated few, but in course of time, it must have come to be used by the ordinary folk. As the language of the local people was Kannada, the Kannada word 'Lingayata' must have been derived from those two Sanskrit words. He states that, such is his explanation, and that he cannot quote an authority on it in the books of the past times. On page 2 he also states that the word 'Lingayata' has been spoken of derisively by some, to denigrate the wearers of Linga.

Professor Sakhare continues - the term 'Veerashaiva is more extensive because it includes Aradhyas who form a class or a community, whereas the term 'Lingayata' does not include the Aradhyas. The Aradhyas call themselves Veerashaivas and not Lingayatas; they profess the practice of Veerashaivism, and in addition they retain some of the Brahminical rites and rituals which are not accepted by the Lingayatas. Professor Sakhare then states that when the terms Veerashaiva and Veerashaivism, and Lingayata and Lingāyatism are used in the book, they are used as coextensive and convertible terms, with the exclusion of the Aradhyas.

Then, under the subtitle 'Shaivism and Veerashaivism' in the same chapter on page 5, the Professor starts by saying that Veerashaivism is a division or a subdivision of Shaivism, and that it is an integral and distinct part of Shaivism. He then states that Veerashaivism has grown out of Shaivism, and has made itself a distinct religious entity, to deserve to be counted and mentioned along with other major religions of the world.

It seems that it is generally accepted that the present day Veerashaivas and

Lingāyatas are the followers of the philosophy and practices put forward in the Kannada vachanas by Basavanna and his contemporary Sharanas of the twelfth century of Common Era. However, the following is to be noted (2):

- The term '**Veerashaiva**' as well as the practicing Veerashaivas existed prior to the 12th century, but their philosophy and practices were based on Shivāgamas and/or Siddhānta Shikhāmaṇi.
- In the commentary on Brahma-sutras called 'Shrīkarabhāshya', Sripatipandita stated that Veerashaiva doctrine is 'Vishēshādvaita'. He referred to Shivāgamas and Siddhānta Shikhāmaṇi but did not refer to Basavanna and his contemporary Sharanas of the twelfth century CE.
- The twelfth century Sharanas revitalized the Veerashaiva Faith, and most practicing Veerashaivas became the followers of the twelfth century Sharana Philosophy.
- Some Veerashaivas continued their previously practiced faith based on the Shivāgamas and /or Siddhānta Shikhāmaṇi.
- The Sharanas of the twelfth century did not give a different name either to the new religious faith, or to its philosophy.
- The Veerashaiva Faith, remained somewhat obscure until the 15th century when it was revived under the Vijayanagara Empire. The revived Veerashaivas are the followers of

the Sharana Philosophy as in Shūnya Sampādane.

- Most of the present day Veerashaivas are the followers of this revived Sharana Philosophy.
- Some who call themselves Veerashaivas continue to practice their faith based on Shivāgamas, Siddhānta Shikhāmaṇi, and/or Srikarabhashya.
- And some Veerashaivas seem to practice a combination of Sharana Philosophy and one or more of the above Sanskrit Philosophies.

- It is generally accepted that the present day **Lingayatas** are the followers of the philosophy and practices put forward in the Kannada vachanas by Basavanna and his contemporary Sharanas of the twelfth century of Common Era.

- The term Lingayata does not come in any literature prior to the 12th century. The origin of the word 'Lingayata' is somewhat obscure, and it is not properly described in religious literature.
- The term 'Lingayata' was used for its literal meaning in a few vachanas of the 12th century. During the Linga initiation ceremony, the Guru places the Ishtalinga on the palm of the disciple and says 'Lingayata'. The meaning of the term 'Lingayata' is said to be 'Linga

comes (to the palm of the disciple)'. At that time, the term was not applicable to the practitioners of the Sharana Philosophy.

- It is said in the Vachanas and Shūnya Sampādane: ***'When the faith in the Ishtalinga obtained through the Guru's grace grows, the Ishtalinga becomes Āyatalinga'.*** *'Āyata'* means *'what has come',* and thus, Āyatalinga means *'What has come is Linga'.* By rearranging the two parts of the term 'Āyata-Linga' in reverse, it becomes 'Linga-āyata' – Lingaayata (Lingāyata).
- The term 'Lingāyata' was not used for the followers of Sharana Philosophy even in the 15th to 17th centuries CE, let alone in the 12th century.
- It seems that the use of the term 'Lingāyata' for the practitioners of Sharana Philosophy came to vogue sometime more recently than the 17th century CE.
- The terms 'Veerashaiva' and 'Lingāyata' have been used interchangeably.

Circumstances in India in the year 1942

India was being ruled by the British. The whole Indian Sub-continent was India which was sometimes referred to as the British India. There was no Pakistan or Bangladesh; they did not exist then. Independence of India from the British was in the year 1947.

In the year 1931, Sir John Marshall, the then Director General of Archaeology of India had published his detailed account of the archaeological findings discovered in the region of the Indus River Valley in a book called 'Mohenjo Daro and Indus Civilization'. In his book, Sir John Marshall had proposed that the period from 3,100 Before Common Era (BCE/BC) to 2,750 BCE was the golden age of Harappa (reference 1, and page 63 of reference 3). It was astonishing to everyone that the findings revealed a very advanced civilization in ancient India during that time. It was astonishing mainly because the European scholars had falsely convinced the whole world that, prior to the so-called Aryan Invasion of India between 1,500 BCE and 1,200 BCE, there was no recognizable civilization in India, and that the people inhabiting ancient India were almost barbarians leading a life of nomads.

This false Theory of Aryan Invasion of India had indicated that the light-skin-colored Indo-European tribes from central Asia had invaded India through the northwest mountain passes of present-day Afghanistan, that the invading Aryans were more civilized, and that Religion, philosophy, literature, and everything else were due to the activities of Aryans after their arrival in India.

This false theory had been invented by European scholars. It was not only not based on any historical records, but also not founded on any archeological evidence. It was based mainly on the linguistic speculation that similarities between Indo-European languages required an original homeland which could not possibly be India itself, but somewhere else (4). The basic fallacy of this theory was the assumption that the ancient people of India could not have on their own, come up with the perfected language of Sanskrit and the Vedas (and come up with a great civilization).

Sir John Marshall in his book states that hitherto it had commonly been supposed that the pre-Aryan people of India were on an altogether lower plane of civilization than their Aryan conquerors, and that to the Aryans, they were much a race so servile and degraded, that they were commonly known as Dasas or slaves (page 7 of reference 1).

This revelation that the so called pre-Aryans, who had been labelled as 'Dravidians', were far more advanced than what was thought to be, was again misinterpreted by the European scholars, who then came up with many new 'Dravidian Invasion' theories, speculating that the native pre-Aryan Dravidians might not have been the original natives but some other people who had come to India at some prior time and had established such advanced civilization. This again assumed that the ancient people of India could not have on their own, establish such an advanced civilization. Many false theories of 'Dravidian Invasion of India' were rampant at the time.

Main Fallacy of the Book

The main fallacy of the book is that Professor Sakhare presumes that the Aryan Invasion theory was factual and does not even raise a single doubt about this invasion, although the theory had been based on the demeaning or insulting assumption that the dark-skin-colored ancient native people of India could not have on their own, come up with an advanced civilization.

Professor Sakhare goes all out on his way to disprove the assumption that the native 'pre-Aryans' were not civilized people, and to disprove the 'Dravidian Invasion' theory. This is well and good, and that it is commendable. But he simply does not go any further and does not raise any doubt about the Aryan invasion theory itself.

The false theory of Aryan invasion of India came about in the 19th century when the British were ruling India. The British scholars discovered the Vedas composed in the beautiful and perfect language of Sanskrit, and they could not believe that the ancient people of India could come up with the Vedas and Sanskrit. They noticed that there were some similarities between Sanskrit and some of the European languages. Instead of considering the possibility that the homeland of these languages could be India itself, and thus looking for the evidence, the European scholars invented this theory, stating that the ancient people of India were uncivilized and therefore could not have come up with the language of Sanskrit and the Vedas.

The British who was ruling India had adamantly asserted that this false theory was factual and taught it in schools as such.

The so-called Pre-Aryan inhabitants of India were labelled as 'Dravidians', who, they claimed, had been driven down to the southern parts of India, mainly to the present-day Tamil Nadu State. They had implicated Tamil as the main language of the Dravidians and had included Kannada and Telugu as other Dravidian languages. Thus, according to the false Aryan Invasion Theory, the uncivilized Dravidians with their Dravidian languages were the ancient inhabitants of India; they were driven down south by the Aryans who invaded India between 1,500 BCE and 1,200 BCE.

The readers should note that all this has been proven to be wrong. There was no Aryan Invasion. The ancient inhabitants of India had been mistakenly labelled as the Dravidians. All the languages of India, including the so-called Dravidian languages of southern India are derived from the original Sanskrit language of India. (references 2, 3, 4, 5, 6, and many more).

If the basic assumption for the theory is wrong, then the theory that is based on that assumption is also wrong. Professor Sakhare, at the time, seems to have had the information to consider the possibility that the Aryan invasion theory itself was wrong.

Not only he was the Sanskrit professor, but also his native language was Kannada. Kannada and Sanskrit languages have the same type of alphabet with the same type of pronunciation; and it is said that there is more than 50% concordance in the words and phrases of the two languages and their meanings. According to the false theory, Kannada, Tamil, and other south Indian languages were the languages of the people in India prior to the arrival of Sanskrit and Vedas which were said to have been brought by the invading Aryans. Then, with the discovery of a far advanced civilization in India around 3,000 BCE, way before the theoretical invasion of Aryans between 1.500 and 1,200 BCE, Professor Sakhare had all the evidence.

Not only that there was a great civilization far more advanced than any other at the time, but also the ancient people of India said to have had the languages like the Sanskrit language. So then, how could that be that the far advanced and civilized ancient people of India with their language like that of Sanskrit, could not have had Sanskrit and the Vedas at that time? It is unfortunate that Professor Sakhare does not even raise a doubt, let alone disprove the Aryan invasion theory.

Refuting Dravidian Invasion Theories

Professor Sakhare devotes his discussion in refuting the various 'Dravidian Invasion' theories. He does the refutation very well at the beginning of the book in fifty-four pages in the second chapter entitled 'Pre-Aryan Dravidian Civilization'. He strongly disputes the previously held belief that the pre-Aryan Dravidians were barbarians leading the life of nomads, and further disputes all the Dravidian Invasion theories, and states that the pre-Aryan Dravidians were the native civilized people of India. This is indeed great and commendable.

At first, Professor Sakhare points out that Sanskrit scholar Muir (page eight of reference 1) differs from others in his opinion that Dravidians were there before the Aryans. Sanskrit scholar Muir opines that Dravidians were an offspring of Aryans. Professor Sakhare states that little credit can be given to this explanation of the origin of the Dravidians.

Professor Sakhare discusses various theories of Dravidian Invasion propounded by many different scholars. Some of those theories are given here.

The theory of the Indo-African-Austral origin of Dravidians and their immigration into India via Lemuria was proposed by Huxley and others and supported by Keene and Morris. According to this theory, once the Indian Ocean was a continent and was called Lemuria. It connected South India to Africa and Australia. Before the submersion of Lemuria, Dravidians entered India from the south.

Sir William Hunter holds that Tibeto-Burmans and Kolarians entered India by the North-eastern passes whereas Dravidians found their way into Punjab by the North-western passes. The two streams crossed each other in central India. Dravidians were stronger and thrust aside the others to east and west, and then settled in the south.

Ragozin proposes the theory of Elamite origin of the Dravidians. There were two hordes of Elamite invaders, one coming by the sea route of the Persian Gulf and settling on the west coast of India, and the other following the land-route through Bolan pass and occupying North India. Professor Sakhare states that this theory seems to have been based on the Puranic myths of deluge and the Ark common to India and Elan.

Professor W. J. Perry says that Egypt was the first home of civilization and Dravidians were a branch of Mediterranean race. It seems to have been based on the resemblance between the Mediterranean people and the so-called Dravidians in the shape of skull, texture of hair, color of eyes, and features and build.

Professor Fleure thinks that immigrants may well have brought to India many improvements not less than one thousand years before the coming of the Aryans, and that Dravidian custom was the result.

Dr. Hall of the British Museum says that Dravidians look like being a Mediterranean people who coming out of Crete and passing through Asia Minor and Mesopotamia, and then coming by the southern part of the Iranian plateau into Sindh whence they came into the interion of India. He says that this must have happened long before 3000 BCE.

Thus, it was said that India was linked more closely to the western world through both the Dravidians and Aryans, and that the west was the cradle of civilization, and that no credit could be given to India for being the home of civilization.

Professor Sakhare says that these theories seem to have sprung from the misconception that India could give no scope climatically or economically for indigenous development of civilization, and that the ancient people of India were a low class of human beings who were twice superseded later by intruders from outside.

Professor Sakhare goes all out on his way to disprove the assumption that the native 'pre-Aryans' were not civilized people, and to disprove the 'Dravidian Invasion' theory. Professor Sakhare says on page eight of his book that the ancient people of India were enjoying an advanced civilization of their own.

To disprove the Dravidian invasion theory, first, Professor Sakhare states that archaeologists agree that nascent civilization of man arose and developed by successive stages of pre-historic times which are broadly divided into Paleolithic, Neolithic, Bronze, and Iron Ages. He states that if enough materials of those different stages and Ages are found in India and developed there by stages, then India would have no cause to look to other countries for importing civilization or customs.

That is the case. It is amply born out by the pre-historic finds collected in India and kept in museums.

Professor Sakhare's eloquent and scholarly discussion in this second chapter includes, among other things, Paleolithic and Neolithic Ages, Bronze and Iron Ages, pottery, art, dress and decorations, occupations, house and buildings, disposal of the dead, Iron Age antiquities, and such. After this scholarly presentation, he states that it may be safely stated that all culture and civilization in India evolved gradually by the people who were inhabitants of ancient India; it is understood that ancient people first evolved a culture in India.

Professor Sakhare then states that his conclusions have been further corroborated and strengthened by the archaeological findings of Mohenjo Daro and Harappa. The Professor says the findings have proved the excellence of an advanced civilization of a people who flourished at the sites of the finds. He further states that a good idea of the advanced condition of civilization can be found from the following extracts from Sir John Marshall's book, and then gives some extracts.

Some extracts from Marshal's book

In the year 1931, Sir John Marshall, the then Director General of Archaeology in India, published a detailed account of the archaeological findings in a book called 'Mohenjo-Daro and Indus Civilization'. In that book, he proposed that the Harappa Age matured during the period from 3,100 BCE to 2,750 BCE.

First, Professor Sakhare gives extracts from the Preface section of Marshall's book and then summarizes it.

Some parts of the extracts from the Preface section of Marshall's book are as follows:

The Archaeological findings exhibit the Indus people of the fourth and third millennia BCE, in possession of a highly developed culture in which no vestige of Indo-Aryan influence is to be found. India is still at the Chalcolithic age – that age in which arms and utensils of stone continue to be used side-by-side with those of copper and bronze.

With the invention of writing, the Indus people were also familiar and employ for this purpose a form of **script** which, though peculiar to India, is evidently analogous to other contemporary scripts of Western Asia and the nearer East.

There is nothing that we know of in pre-historic Egypt or Mesopotamia or anywhere else in Western Asia to compare with the well-built baths and commodious houses of the citizens of Mohenjo-Daro.

Equally peculiar to the Indus valley and stamped with an individual character of their own are its art and its religion. Nothing that we know of bears any resemblance.

Their religion is so characteristically Indian as hardly to be distinguishable from the still living Hinduism. None perhaps is more remarkable than this discovery that **Shaivism has a history going back to the chalcolithic Age (4,300 BCE to 3,300 BCE) or perhaps even further still, and that it thus takes its place as the most ancient living faith in the world.**

One thing that stands out clear and unmistakable is that the civilization hitherto revealed is not an incipient civilization, but one already age-old and stereotyped on Indian soil, with many millennia of human endeavor behind it. Thus, India must henceforth be recognized as one of the most important areas where the civilization process of society was initiated and developed.

Professor Sakhare then summarizes the Preface section of Sir John Marshall's book.

Next, Professor Sakhare states that the Indus people were in communication with other parts of India, particularly South India, and with other parts of the world. They carried on trade with the people there for the supply of material required. This, he says will be evident from the following extracts, and quotes from the main part of Marshall's book.

Much of the gold of Mohenjo Daro and Harappa is alloyed with substantial percentage of silver, and this alloy is found in Kolar Gold Fields of Mysore (present day Karnataka), and at Anantapur in Madras (present day Tamil Nadu), but not in other districts from which the Indus people would have been likely to procure it.

The green Amazon stone almost certainly came from Nilgiris hills. The nearest spot from which the beautiful green amazon stone (a variety of feldspar) could be got was Dodbetta in the Nilgiris, far away in South India.

The above notable excerpts clearly make the point that the great ancient civilization of India was not localized to the Indus River Valley but was in all parts of India.

Professor Sakhare on page 51 of his book rightfully makes the following statement: It has been an error to call the civilization discovered at Mohenjo Daro, Harappa, and other sites, 'The Indus Valley Civilization', for this phrase seems to suggest that such civilization flourished in the Indus Valley only. It was not localized to this area only; it was all over India and Ceylon (present day Sri Lanka).

This following part of extract from page 42 of Marshall's book given on page 42 also of Sakhare's book is very disturbing – 'Of the languages of these (Indus Valley) texts, little more can be said at present than that there is no reason for connecting it in any way with Sanskrit; the Indus Civilization was pre-Aryan, and the Indus language or languages must be pre-Aryan also'. It is unfortunate that, such a scholar as Sir John Marshall is, even after gloriously describing the advanced civilization of ancient India, continues to adamantly hold his support for the Aryan invasion theory which was based on the fallacy that the ancient people of India could not have, on their own come up with such a perfected Sanskrit Language and the Vedas. The readers may note that the Indus Valley glyphs (script/texts) found at the archaeological excavations of Mohenjo Daro and Harappa have been proven to be pre-Brahmi script of Sanskrit.

On the same page Marshall states – 'Western Alpine (some Europeans) are said to be strongly represented among the Kanarese-speaking (Kannada-speaking) peoples of Western Deccan and Mysore (present day Karnataka State), but if the racial characteristics can be taken into account in this problem of language, it is clearly the long headed Mediterraneans who have strongest claim to a connection by blood with the Dravidians and are most likely to have used a Dravidian speech'.

Not recognizing Sanskrit as the original language of India

Professor Sakhare on page 45 of his book states as follows: 'Proto-Dravidian language naturally resembles Hale-Kannada (old-Kannada) more closely than modern Kannada. Similarly, it is nearer to Sangam Tamil than to modern Tamil. In this proto-Dravidian language (unrecognized Sanskrit), the construction of the phrase is generally the same as the modern Dravidian languages (Kannada, Tamil, Telugu, and Malayalam). It is commendable that Professor Sakhare noticed this. But, if Professor Sakhare was able to discern that Kannada and Sanskrit were similar languages, then why did he not think that Sanskrit was also the language of the ancient people of India?

Furthermore, Professor Sakhare states that he deciphered about one thousand eight hundred inscriptions found at the archaeologic sites. Of all these, there are three signs in the so-called Dravidian languages which evidently represent fish. He says if we suppose that the languages of Mohenjo-Daro were Sanskrit and we read the three above signs Matsya or even

MINA – these two words in Sanskrit have no other meaning than fish. It is unfortunate that, even then, Professor Sakhare did not think that Sanskrit was also the language of the ancient people of India.

On page 51 of his book, Professor Sakhare makes this comment: The script of Mohenjo-Dro is a script of such a logical nature that it may be at times read without knowing its meaning. He says that when the Aryans entered India, they had no script of their own and they adopted the Dravidian script. This script (unrecognized Sanskrit) developed into two different channels, one northern and the other southern. Such is the origin of the two of North and South India, from which all modern Indian alphabets proceed. Despite this Aryan-Dravidian divide, Professor Sakhare is describing the Sanskrit language.

Karnataka and Mohenjo Daro

Professor Sakhare discusses the connection between the peoples of Karnataka and Mohenjo Daro in this second chapter under the sub-heading 'Karnataka and Mohenjo Daro'. Other connections between the two have already been stated above.

Professor Sakhare states that the connection between Karnataka and Mohenjo Daro is more explicit than the general interrelation mentioned above.

Professor Sakhare mentions that the people of Karnataka are referred to in one of the seal inscriptions of Mohenjo Daro as one of the ancient tribes of the land. The sign reads *Kaṇanir.* He says its Sanskrit modification is Kannadigas which refers to the people of modern Karnataka State.

Professor Sakhare also mentions a second inscription which he calls as 'the fragment of extraordinary literary beauty.' It refers to the people of Coorg (a region in the Karnataka State) as Kuda-gas; their language is still called 'Kodagu'.

Professor Sakhare continues, and states that besides the above two forms, there is still the form in 'ru' which is purely Kannada; by adding the sound of 'ru' the plural is obtained representing the pleural objects.

The Lingayata connection

Professor Sakhare, continuing the Karnataka and Mohenjo Daro connection makes a specific reference to a sign - a sign that is common to the present day Lingayatas and the inscriptions of Harappa and Mohenjo Daro. The modern Lingayatas of the Kannada country depict a sign on the walls of their homes. This sign is often found in the inscriptions of Mohenjo Daro and Harappa. The sign reads *'kūḍu',* and it means 'union', the 'union' which is so predominant in the religious tenets of Veerashaiva sect.

This Veerashaiva connection is an important point to note. There is no doubt that the archaeologic findings indicate the existence of Shaivism at the time. But here, Professor Sakhare is making a strong point for the existence of the concepts of Veerashaivas at the time. The point is taken very well. This so-called pre-Aryan Dravidian time according to Professor Sakhare, is now well established to be that of the Vedic period of the Āryas (there is no 'n' at the end of the word), not of the Dravidians or Aryans of the now defunct Aryan Invasion Theory.

False Invasion Story

Professor Sakhare states that the Aryans came to India from the banks of Volga and arrived at Kathiawar in India. This according to him is established:

This story begins on page 55 of his book. The Aryans coming from the banks of Volga River, in their migration eastwards, had stopped for a long time in Mesopotamia. The migration of a whole nation to their new land, though promising, had innumerable perils. When the rude and uncivilized Aryans encountered the wonderful natural goods or manufactured products brought by the Panis, the civilized people from India, who were coming seafaring from the 'country of the Sun' which was later called Saurashtra and then Kathiawar on the western coast of India.

- It is to be noted here that Professor Sakhare states that Aryans were rude and uncivilized and that the ancient people of India were civilized with wonderful, manufactured products. If that is the case, how could the uncivilized Aryans possibly bring such beautifully perfected Sanskrit and Rigveda to the civilized India with perfected languages such as Kannada which is like Sanskrit?

Professor Sakhare continues: Aryans had never seen the sea and could not have any seafaring inclinations. Migration of the whole nation of the Aryans from Mesopotamia to India would have innumerable perils. Therefore, the leader of the Aryans, the Asura Indar called Indra [yes, Indra, that is what the Professor states], as a trial took two families – the families of Yadus and Turvasas – with him and set sail in one of the ships of the Panis and landed several days later, on the shores of Kathiawar.

Professor Sakhare states that the first expedition of the Aryans into India across the ocean is mentioned several times in the Rigveda, and then gives two quotations without giving the actual Rigveda references: *"What time, O Hero, o'er the sea thou broughtest, in safety broughtest them; O hero thou keepest Turvasa and Yadu safely."* And *"So sapient Indra, lord of might, brought Turvasa and Yadu, those who feared the flood in safety o'er".*

- It is to be pointed out to the readers that these two quotations do not describe the first expedition of the Aryans into India; there was no expedition. It is astonishing that Professor Sakhare, being the Sanskrit professor misinterprets the Rigveda verses. Nowhere in Rigveda there is anything about the foreigners invading India. His story seems ridiculous.

Then Professor Sakhare states, on page 58, that the discussions he presented about evolution of the advanced civilization of the ancient people of India, make it clear that man arose in India, simultaneously if he arose in other parts of the world as well, in pre-historic times and gradually developed a culture in all its stages and ages. It is to be noted that, at present, the scientific evidence indicates that the anatomically modern humans originated in Africa, that there were no parallel evolutionary origins, and that all non-African people are descendants of the anatomically modern humans of Africa (5).

Professor Sakhare continues: 'Scholars generally trace the origin and growth of Religion, Philosophy, and Literature in India to the Vedas. According to them there was nothing in India before the coming of the Aryans to India which was then a land occupied by people uncivilized and barbarous. The Aryans, they say, brought with them some civilization which they spread among people of India after conquering them. But even the references made in the Vedas to the people already there shows that they with whom the Aryans had to fight, were a people rich in wealth and cattle, who owned chariots and had weapons which they used in fights with the Aryans. The rise of the Aryan did not alter the stage of culture reached by the people'. As evidence for this, Professor Sakhare gives Rigveda references, and then states:

"*This wrong idea of scholars firmly rooted in their minds made them blind to the references in the Rigveda made to the people and their enviable condition of living and then tried to interpret the references to suit their wrong idea of pre-Aryan people of India".*

Here, Professor Sakhare recognizes the mistake made by the European scholars, but he does not think of the possibility that there was no Aryan invasion of India. Therefore, the same could be said about Professor Sakhare –

that the wrong idea of the Aryan invasion of India firmly rooted in his mind made him blind to the references, and he tried to interpret the reference to suit this wrong idea that the Dravidians and the Aryans were two separate races with separate religions, languages, and cultures – such a sorry situation indeed.

Professor Sakhare then states: 'The face-type of the average Indian of today is same as that of his Dravidian ancestors of thousands of years ago. Among the modern Indians, the ancient pre-Aryan type of the head has survived, while that of the Aryan conqueror died out long ago'. Again, Professor Sakhare disregards this evidence which indicates that there was never an Aryan invasion of India.

Discussion on Shaivism

In the first chapter of the book, Professor Sakhare states that Veerashaivism is a distinct religious entity that has grown out of Shaivism, and that to understand how Veerashaivism has evolved out of Shaivism, it is indispensable to study and trace the growth of Shaivism historically. Accordingly, he devotes seven of the fifteen chapters in his book to the discussion pertinent to Shaivism.

'Shaivism, the Dravidian Religion'

The third chapter in the book is entitled 'Shaivism, the Dravidian Religion'. The Professor's wrong conviction, that there was Aryan invasion of India, and the people living in India prior to this supposed invasion were called 'Dravidians', continues to skew his discussions so that some of his discussions become superfluous.

Professor Sakhare states that - one full chapter has been devoted to religion of Sindh people by Sir John Marshall in his book 'Mohenjo Daro and Indus Civilization' where he has concluded that those people worshipped mother Goddess and a male deity

Shiva, as represented on seals, images, carvings, and other signs discovered in different sites; but Marshall's conclusions may not be considered very authoritative, because, the inscriptions on the seals are not satisfactorily explained by him. Then he states that Father Heras has given such satisfactory explanation, and that his reading of the inscriptions proves beyond the shadow of doubt that Shiva and Shakti were the chief deities of Mohenjo Daro people (who have been labelled 'Dravidians'). Then, on pages 62 through 76, Professor Sakhare goes over his own interpretation of the 'Dravidian Religion'.

Professor Sakhare gives a story of what he thinks happened; the following is an excerpt from his book on pages 76 and 77.

"Centuries of years ago, the Aryans were a wandering race and moved from place to place with their cattle in search of permanent place of residence. But their nomadic tendency came to an end when they arrived in India, which they found expansive and convenient, and which afforded all facilities geographically and economically for the propagation of their race. They at once made up their mind to settle there. India, they found suitable in every way and saw that it was too charming to be left in preference to another. But they did not find it quite easy to do so. The Dravidians were already there, who being the original inhabitants and masters of the land, could not naturally brook the idea of the Aryan intruders settling there and did not like to allow the alien immigrants to settle... The Aryans, therefore, had no easy task of settling in India. The Dravidians tried their utmost to drive back the intruding Aryans out of India; and racial pride raised, naturally of course, a barrier between the immigrants and the original inhabitants. But the Aryans, strong-willed and tenacious, did not and could not afford to yield to the resistance and attempts of the Dravidians to drive them out. The Aryans had to struggle and struggle hard for their existence in India..."

Then Professor Sakhare states that Rigveda is the evidence for the above story.

- The readers should note that Rigveda does not have that story, and there is no such evidence. Rigveda, as translated by the scholars H. H. Wilson (7), Ralph T. H. Griffith (8), and many others, including the Indian scholars, does not have that story.

Furthermore, the Vachana literature and the Sanskrit books he refers to in his statement on page xii under Argument, "Though I am positively of the opinion that Vachana Shastra is the basic literature of the religion as its scriptures, I have based all my thesis with profuse quotations on Sanskrit books for the simple reason that my thesis centers round a Sanskrit work" also do not have any story about Aryan invasion of India. There is nothing about any Aryan invasion in all the Indian literature and the world literature that is prior to this wrong invention of the theory of Aryan Invasion of India.

Professor Sakhare continues – 'The religion of the Aryans was altogether different from that of the Dravidians whose religion stood on a higher plane, and hence great was the clash and conflict between the two races in India as recorded and told by the Vedas'.

- It is to be noted that Vedas do not make such statement (7, 8). The original false theory of Aryan Invasion of India had falsely stated that there was no recognizable religion in India prior to the Aryans' arrival. But then with the archaeological findings that India had a great civilization with its own culture and religion, the Professor Sakhare, instead of doubting the theory itself, brings up the two different religions and the Aryan-Dravidian divide.

Professor Sakhare then states that the Aryans called themselves 'Āryas' (pronounced as Aaryas), and spoke of Dravidians contemptuously as Dasyus, Dasas, Panis, and such.

Please note that Professor Sakhare continues to misinterpret what Rigveda says. It is somewhat discomforting, because he is a Sanskrit Professor, and is misinterpreting Vedic Sanskrit.

- The following is to be reiterated here: The word 'Aryan', with an 'n' at the end, is an English word; it was invented in the 19th century CE. There were no Aryans. The word 'Aryan' or the Aryan people, and the word 'Dravidian' or the Dravidian people are not found in the Vedas or in any other literature that existed prior to that false theory. The Sanskrit word 'Ārya' is in the Vedas, particularly in the Rigveda. It does not have an 'n' at the end. 'Ārya' means 'noble' or 'cultured'. The word Ārya does not indicate a race. The ancient inhabitants of India who transmitted the sacred heritage of the Vedas, described themselves as Āryas (3). There is nothing in the Vedas that says that these 'Āryas' are foreigners or that they invaded India from somewhere else. The conflicts that are in the Vedas were the internal conflicts.

- The readers should note that Rigveda portrays non-violence and humility and surrender to the Gods and sages. It includes the kings as an important aspect of the greater teaching. Kings protect the sacrifice and guard the spiritual life of the Aryas. Their battles are portrayed as a struggle between good and evil, truth and falsehood, or spirituality and materialism. The kings follow the wisdom of their ruling priests. In this regard the kings protect the Āryas who followed the spiritual culture of the seers. Those among the same people, who did not follow the spiritual rules were the fallen Āryas. Many of these fallen Āryas were reinstated as Āryas once they purified themselves and started following the spiritual Vedic rules. Some who did not were driven away by the kings (6).

- Dasyus, Panis, and some others were the materialistic fallen Āryas. Dasyus or Dasas are described as destroyers of rites, and Panis are portrayed in Rigveda as being very rich in gold, cattle and horses (page 119 of reference 6). The conflict described in Rigveda is a conflict between the spiritual and the non-spiritual materialistic people.

However, it is to be pointed out that Professor Sakhare correctly translates some parts of Rigveda, but he misinterprets what that means. On page 79, for example, he states as follows: 'The hymns of the Rigveda contain numerous references to persons, apparently of different descriptions, who were either hostile or indifferent to the system of religious worship, which the Rishis, the seers of Vedic Mantras, professed and inculcated. There is a long list of condemnatory epithets to persons, such as godless, without rites, without Indra, revilers of gods, without devotion, un-sacrificing, followers of other rites, and such.'

The above passage describes the fallen Āryas who were indifferent or hostile to the system of religious worship professed by the seers. Professor Sakhare is calling these people the Dravidians in contradiction to his own statement that the Dravidians were a far advanced people, more advanced than the invading Aryans. Many passages given there show this type of correct translation and then wrong interpretation.

Regarding the worship of Rudra in Rigveda, Professor Sakhare, on page 83, states that although Rudra was borrowed from the Dravidians, there was no opposition from the Aryans for its adoption, and that the adoration of Rudra in Rigveda was regarded as an innovation. The readers should note that there were no Aryans or Dravidians; everyone was 'Ārya'. The ancient people of India were the Āryas. There was no borrowing or adoption in Rigveda. The beginning of the Rigveda period was around 10,000 BCE, and the Vedic period had been well established by 3,100 BCE.

Professor Sakhare, on page 84, states that it would be more correct to describe the Indian Religion as Dravidian religion stimulated and modified by the ideas of foreign invaders. Then on page 90, he concludes the third chapter by stating that Aryans borrowed not only the Dravidian gods but also their religious philosophy. The readers should note that there was no Dravidian or Aryan religion; it was all the religion of the 'Ārya'; it was just the Religion of India.

'Shaivism during the Vedic times'

In the fourth chapter entitled 'Shaivism during the Vedic times', Professor Sakhare starts by stating – after having established that Shaivism was a pre-Aryan and a Dravidian religion, the discussion now proceeds to see how Shaivism fared during Vedic times when the Aryan religion and culture prevailed and predominated.

It is to be noted that, because Professor Sakhare believes in the false Aryan invasion theory, he is presuming the Vedic time to be after 1,500 BCE or 1,200 BCE. The Aryan invasion theory has been disproven; there was no Aryan invasion ever. Most scholars now believe that the beginning of the Rigveda period was 10,000 BCE, and that the Vedic period had peaked between 3,100 BCE and 2,700 BCE. The Harappa and Mohenjo Daro findings were of that period.

It is very comforting to note that Professor Sakhare sets the record straight as to what Rigveda says about Rudra. He states:

'It can be easily seen, when the hymns of Rigveda addressed to Rudra are carefully analyzed, that twofold functions are attributed to Rudra – that of bestowing prosperity, and that of destroying suffering'.

Professor Sakhare categorically states that the idea that Rudra is a god of terror will have to be dismissed. He points the finger at Muir and Weber who falsely claim that idea. That is brave indeed. And then Professor Sakhare states that, in Rigveda, Rudra is considered as a benevolent divinity when Rudra confers wealth and welfare and is considered as a wrathful divinity when Rudra punishes evil doers. **Bravo!**

Then Professor Sakhare states that there are many indications in Rigveda that go to prove that Rudra of Rigveda is the Shiva of later times. Although his statement here is true, it is to be noted that Professor Sakhare is ambiguous. He was insisting that Shiva was what the so-called pre-Aryan Dravidians were worshipping before even the Vedas and

Aryans existed based on his false belief on the disproven theory of Aryan invasion of India. If that was the case, Shiva would have already been there prior to Rudra of Rigveda.

Professor Sakhare continues his discussion pertinent to Rudra-Shiva that is found in all the Vedas including the Upanishads. He discusses how Rudra-Shiva became the Parabrahman of the Upanishads. Then he discusses the point that Shvetāshvatara Upanishad establishes Rudra-Shiva to be the theistic Brahman, instead of the non-theistic Absolute Brahman of the other principal Upanishads. Indeed, all this is commendable.

'Development of Shaivism in later times up to the 12th century AD'

In the fifth chapter entitled 'Development of Shaivism in later times up to the 12th century AD (CE)', Professor Sakhare discusses Shaivism aspects in the Sutras (Shrutis) and Smritis, Ramayana and Mahabharata epics, and in the Puranas. He also discusses Shaivism during the period of 63 Nayanars. The Nayanars lived during the period from the 4th to the 9th century CE.

During that period, Shaivism flourished and became firmly established in south India. The Nayanars translated Sanskrit Shivāgamas into Tamil Shiva doctrines. This is all well and good.

'Shaivism, a pre-Vaishnava religion'

In the sixth chapter called 'Shaivism, a pre-Vaishnava religion', Professor Sakhare says that Rudra-Shiva was not a sectarian god, and that worship of Vishnu was a later development. Because of his misconception, he states that Shiva was a Dravidian god before Aryans invaded India, and that God Vishnu was a later development.

'Rise of the Agamas, their development and contents'

The seventh chapter is titled 'Rise of the Agamas, their development and contents'. Professor Sakhare raises **three questions** and then tries to answer them.

The first one is to do with the age of the Āgamas. He states that the age of the Agamas can be determined from the references to the Agamas in various works. He goes over 14 works going back from the recent to the earliest references starting with the 16th century work. He then gives some notable references - Kalidasa's Raghuvamsha (first century BCE) refers to Agamas; various Puranas mention the Agamas; Mahabharata indirectly refers to Agamas; in Maitrayaniyopanishad Agamic literature is referred to twice; the Shvetāshvatara Upanishad is certainly an Agamic Upanishad, later followed by other Agamic Upanishads like Atharva-Shira and Kaivalya; the Bhagavad-Gita itself seems to have been written under the influence of Agamas.

Then he makes a statement: '*The Gita like the Shvetāshvatara Upanishad, is in complete accord with the Agamas but opposed to the Vedas and the Upanishads*'.

- First, Shvetāshvatara Upanishad is part of the Veda. It belongs to Krishna Yajurveda. How can it be opposed to the Veda and to the Upanishads? Whatever it states is part of the statement of the Vedas. Second, Bhagavad-Gita is not opposed to the Vedas and the Upanishads. Bhagavad-Gita is said to be the essence of the Upanishads.

Professor Sakhare states that very many passages of the Bhagavad-Gita differ very little from various Agamic passages, and gives about 44 passages of the two, side by side, to show that the Bhagavad-Gita verses are like the Agamic passages. He states that, the contention that Agamas themselves must have borrowed from the Gita cannot stand because, Shri Krishna, the author of Gita, was himself a devotee of Shiva and said to have learnt spiritual philosophy from Shiva. The readers may very well know that such reasoning will not stand scrutiny.

- Please note that Bhagavad-Gita is a small part of Mahabharata, and it was composed by Veda Vyasa prior to the year 3000 BCE. The oldest Āgamas were probably composed at the time of the Āraṇyakas sometime more recent than the year 2700 BCE, and newer Āgamas were composed as late as the year 800 CE. Therefore, Bhagavad-Gita came first and then the Āgamas. (There was no Aryan invasion of India.)

Then on page 167, Professor Sakhare states the following: *"Even though the Gita seems to have borrowed from the Upanishads, overall, it seems to be rather opposed to the*

Upanishads in its tone and trend, and to be more in consonance with the teachings of the Agamas. Firstly, the Gita itself condemns the Vedas in no uncertain terms, as will be evident from what it says." And then he gives four verses from Bhagavad-Gita in Sanskrit only without giving the actual numbers for the verses, and without translating the verses into English. It is to be pointed out to the readers that throughout the book Sanskrit texts from various references are given, and not translated into English. These Bhagavad-Gita verses are II.42, II.43, II.46, and II.53. The translation given below is taken from reference numbers 9 and 10.

The unwise who delight in the flowery words disputing about the Vedas say that there is nothing other than this (material enjoyment). II.42

The desire-ridden hold the attainment of heaven as the goal of birth and its activities; their words are laden with specific rites bringing in pleasure and power. II.43 (then 2 verses are skipped).

To an enlightened Brahmana all the Vedas are as useful as a reservoir of water for irrigation when there is flood everywhere. II.46 (then six verses are skipped).

When your intellect which had been tossed about by the conflicting opinions of the Vedas, becomes poised and firmly fixed in equilibrium, then you shall get into yoga. II.53

The readers should note that there is nothing in the above verses to make such an outrageous statement that 'the Gita itself condemns the Vedas in no uncertain terms' (refutation of all this is given below). Professor Sakhare, then takes two Sanskrit words from the Bhagavad-Gita verse II.42 and one word from verse II.53, and states that the words say the following: the word *'vedavadaratah'* warns people against concerting themselves with the Vedic lore and teachings; the word *'nanyadastitivadinah'* means that the Upanishads' attaining the position equal to the Vedas is denied by some; and the word *'shrutivipratipanna'* wants people not to be distracted or misled by the Vedas. Then Professor Sakhare states "*That is to say, the Gita wants people to give up the Vedas and devote themselves to the Agamas".* The readers should note that the Gita does not say such things.

Refutation of Professor Sakhare's statement about Bhagavad-Gita

There is no dispute that there are many commonalities between the Agamas and the Bhagavad-Gita. What is disconcerting is that Professor Sakhare, being a professor of Sanskrit, makes these statements. First, Bhagavad-Gita itself states that it is the essence of the Upanishads as follows:

Bhagavad-Gita begins with the *'Gita Dhyāna'* which means 'Meditation on Gita'. This meditation has seven verses. The fourth verse says something like this: "All the Upanishads are the cows, the one who milks the cows is Krishna, Arjuna is the calf, people of intellect are the drinkers, and the milk is the supreme nectar of the Gita". It basically says that Bhagavad-Gita is the essence of the Upanishads. Furthermore, in the colophon at the end of each chapter, The Bhagavad-Gita refers to itself as an Upanishad – 'In the Upanishad of Bhagavad-Gita, the knowledge of Brahman, the Science of Yoga...'

The fundamentals of the Vedic philosophy are in the Upanishads, and the essence of the Upanishads is the Bhagavad-

Gita. The emphasis in Bhagavad-Gita is on Karma Yoga, the path of non-selfish action. This is somewhat of a departure from the Upanishadic teaching that prefers the path of Jnana Yoga, the path of discriminative Knowledge. This may be because the Upanishads were geared specifically to those already free from social obligations – the forest dwellers and the sannyasis, whereas the Bhagavad-Gita is intended for the society at large, the Karma Yoga being relevant to the householder as well as to the monastic. It should be noted that the Bhagavad-Gita does not condemn the Vedas.

Professor Sakhare has taken the above four verses of Bhagavad-Gita out of context and that too not in one order. Furthermore, he is misinterpreting what these verses say, and misleading the readers. It is appalling that he is doing that. The following two paragraphs give the meaning of the verses from the verse II.41 to verse II.53 taken from references 9 and 10:

Those who are resolute have only one thought of Self-knowledge; but those who are not firm in their mind have thoughts that are endless and branched. The unwise who delight in flowery words disputing about the Vedas say that there is nothing other than this material enjoyment. The desire-ridden hold the attainment of heaven as the goal of birth and its activities; their words are laden with specific rites and rituals bringing in pleasure and power. There is no fixity of mind for those who cling to pleasure and power and whose judgment is obscured by such ritualistic activities. Vedas enumerate the three guṇas of mind; one has to transcend the three guṇas and be free from the pairs of opposites (dualities), be ever balanced and un-concerned with the thoughts of acquisition and hoarding; one has to be centered in the Self. **To an enlightened person, the Vedas are as useless as a reservoir of water for irrigation when there is flood everywhere.**

One should seek to perform one's own duty without seeking any claim on one's rewards. The fruit of work should not be the motive for action. And one should not lean towards inaction either. One should perform action renouncing attachments and fixing the mind in Yoga. Being even minded in success and failure, the equilibrium is verily Yoga.

Work done with selfish motives is far inferior to that performed in equanimity of mind; wretched are the result seekers; take refuge in the evenness of mind. The one fixed in equanimity of mind, frees oneself in life from vice and virtue alike; therefore, one should devote oneself to Yoga. Work done to perfection is verily Yoga. The wise, imbued with evenness of mind, renouncing the fruits of their action, freed from fetters of birth, verily go to the divine state. When one's understanding transcends the veil of delusion, then one will become indifferent to what is heard and what is yet to be heard. When one's intellect which had been tossed about by the conflicting opinions of the Vedas, becomes poised and firmly fixed in equilibrium, then one gets into Yoga.

In the above passages, Bhagavad-Gita does not condemn the Vedas in general. It condemns the ritualistic part of the Vedas, the people who perform these rituals, and the conflicting message the Vedas portray. As the readers very well know, the Vedas in general are divided into two parts - the first ritualistic action-oriented part that includes part of the Samhitas and the Brahmanas, and the second part which is the knowledge-oriented part of the Vedas that includes the Upanishads. The two parts of the Vedas give some conflicting messages. Bhagavad-Gita, which is the essence of the Upanishads, is saying that one should disregard the ritualistic part of the Vedas and the conflicting opinions there off, concentrate on stabilizing the mind to get into Yoga. It may be said that Bhagavad-Gita does not like the Vedas in general and ritualistic parts of the Vedas in particular, but it is to be noted that, it is not opposed to the Upanishads which are part of the Vedas.

Continuing, Professor Sakhare concludes on the first topic concerning the age of the Āgamas by stating that the beginnings of the Āgamas go back to the time of the Āraṇyakas. Most scholars agree with his statement. But Professor Sakhare is ambiguous. Although his statement is true, he does not give an approximate date for this time of the Āraṇyakas. The reason why Professor Sakhare does not give a date is not clear. If he had to give one, because he believed in the false theory of the Aryan invasion of India, it would have to be a date way more recent than 1,200 BCE. But because

Professor Sakhare insists that Shaivism was the religion of the highly civilized Pre-Aryan people, and its philosophy is based on the Āgamas, then the Āgamas should have existed way prior to Āraṇyakas, and that too way prior to any part of the Vedas. Vedas constitute Samhitas, Brahmanas, Āraṇyakas, and Upanishads. Now that the Aryan invasion theory has been disproven, most scholars give the date for the beginning of the time of the Āraṇyakas to be around 2,700 BCE, and therefore, the beginnings of the Āgamas go back to the time of the Āraṇyakas around 2,700 BCE.

The second topic is the origin and source of the Āgamas. Professor Sakhare gives three theories – one is that Āgamas arose out of the Brahmanas and thus were contemporaneous with the Āraṇyakas; the second is that Āgamas interpret the Upanishads and elaborate their teachings; and the third is that the Āgamas are an independent literature and in no way relate to the Vedas. Professor Sakhare, after giving his own long explanation, sides with the third theory. However, he notes, on page 176, that the later thinkers hold that the Āgamas and the Vedas are one and the same. But he thinks that the Āgamas and the Vedas are two different streams of thought running in two parallel channels acting and reacting upon each other to ultimately blend indistinguishably. Then on the same page he asks a question and answers – 'What is then the source of the Āgamas? We (it is not clear who he means when he says 'we', it probably just means I for himself) maintain in reply that the pre-Aryan Dravidian culture and religion was the source of the Āgamas'. There is no dispute that the source of the Āgamas was the culture that existed around 3,000 BCE. But Professor Sakhare calls that culture the pre-Aryan Dravidian culture which was really the Vedic culture of the Āryas (not Aryans); there were no Aryans or Dravidians; they were all just Āryas, the ancient, civilized people of India. It is to be noted that Professor Sakhare continues to build his case for two different races and two different religions – Dravidian and Aryan - somewhat in a biased way.

The third topic is the contents of the Āgamas. It is very briefly stated that the Āgamas are divided into four parts called padas - Kriya, Charya, Yoga, and Jnana - the

Kriya-pada is said to embody all acts such as preparing the ground, laying the foundation for the temple and establishing the idol. Then Professor Sakhare states that, during the early period, the Āgamas pertained to the three main agamic cults, namely, Shaiva, Shakta, and Vaishnava; and that the religion of the present-day Hindus has long been wholly Agamic. There is more discussion of the Agamas under topics pertinent to Lingāyatism.

The last statement Professor Sakhare makes in this chapter is that the religion of the present-day Hindus has long been wholly Agamic. This statement is contrary to what he states at the beginning of the fourth chapter. There, Professor Sakhare states that the Aryan religion and culture prevailed and predominated. If that is the case, then, the present-day Hindus would be practicing the Aryan religion which is said to have been based on the Vedas. He has been trying to make a case for two separate religions – one a Dravidian religion with Agamas being its literature; and the other the Aryan religion with Vedas being its literature. The readers very well know by now that everything is really one religion, the religion of the Āryas which is the religion of the Hindus.

'The meaning of Shivalinga'

The eighth chapter is titled 'The meaning of Shivalinga'. Shivalinga is the symbol that represents Shiva. The term is usually applied to the Sthavara (stationary) Linga installed in the Shiva temples. Professor Sakhare at the beginning of the chapter states that there is much misunderstanding regarding Shivalinga; there is a deep-rooted prejudice which considers Shivalinga to be a phallus symbol. Later in this chapter he states that the root-cause of this deep prejudice and misunderstanding lies in the idea and the gratuitous assumption that the Dravidians, at the time of the Aryan invasion of India were merely a primitive people with no civilizations of their own. Professor Sakhare, rightfully, dispels this misunderstanding and condemns the impure notion of the well-known European writers.

Hurray!

Ishtalinga

Chapter nine is titled 'Ishtalinga and Image Worship'. This chapter has only 3 pages and is interposed here under the discussion of Shaivism probably to compare the Ishtalinga to the Shivalinga which is discussed above in the previous chapter.

Professor Sakhare states that Ishtalinga is the Linga worn on the body, and then he describes how Ishtalinga is made. He compares it to Shivalinga that is worshipped in the temples. Shivalinga is an image of Shiva, and therefore, its worship is an image worship. He then emphatically states that **Ishtalinga worship is not an image worship because Ishtalinga is not an image of Shiva, it is Shiva itself. Therefore, the worship of Ishtalinga is not an image worship, it is the direct worship of Shiva.**

He continues. In the scheme of Shatsthala Philosophy, Linga is the manifested Shiva (Saguna Shiva), and anga is the devotee of a human being, and the two are only the twofold manifestations of Nirguna Shiva (Shiva with no attributes); therefore, Linga and anga are one and the same.

Professor Sakhare then discusses different modes of worship in general. He states that, although there is no scriptural sanction behind it, some Lingayatas do image-worship at home; it is merely an imitation of the image worship of other Hindus which is universal in India. It is indeed great that he makes this important point.

In this chapter he just mentions that the Ishtalinga is given to a child as soon as it is born, to be worn on the body throughout life, and to be buried with the dead body upon death. He does not mention that Guru gives the Ishtalinga during initiation ceremony. He concludes this chapter by stating that the custom of image-worship is an abnormal growth on the Lingayata religion and has sapped the life and spirit of the religion. Well said.

Continuation of discussion on Shaivism

'Schools of Shaivism'

The tenth chapter is titled 'Schools of Shaivism'. Professor Sakhare starts with a definition of a 'sect': 'A sect is a religious body or denomination, in which distinct religious doctrines and principles are formulated and which has a distinct religious philosophy and common forms of worship that distinguishes one particular sect from another, either of the same religion or another religion'.

Professor Sakhare then states that the philosophy and practice of Shaivism have been set forth in very general terms in Shvetāshvatara Upanishad, but in the Atharva-Shira-Upanishad it is found to have attained a more definite form; in the Atharva-Shira-Upanishad there occur the special technical terms of Shaivism which are common to all different sects that arise later from Shaivism. It is indeed interesting to note that, although there is no disagreement on this statement, it is surprising that Professor Sakhare is admitting to the Vedic origin of Shaivism, and that there is no Aryan-Dravidian divide.

Professor Sakhare describes different sects of Shaivas and describes the 36 tattvas (principles) in detail. In addition, he describes the commonalities as well as the differences between Shaivism and Shaktism.

It is to be noted here that on page xi under 'Argument', Professor Sakhare states that Shaivism, Shaktism and Lingāyatism are all allied religions; the basic philosophy is the same except that in Shaktism Shakti is considered prominent, whereas, in Shaivism and Lingāyatism, Shiva is considered primary. But then he states there: "But Lingāyatism is more allied to Shaktism". Why he makes such a statement is not clear.

In the first chapter of his book Professor Sakhare states 'Veerashaivism is a division or a sub-division of Shaivism, and that it is an integral and distinct part of Shaivism. Veerashaivism has grown out of Shaivism...' Then he, himself, has seven of the fifteen chapters of his book devoted to Shaivism and in addition he incorporates philosophy and practices of Shaivism into the chapter on philosophy and practice of Lingāyatism to show that they are similar. That is almost half of this book devoted to Shaivism. With all this, why he makes such an unacceptable statement as above without explaining any further is disturbing. The readers should note that the Veerashaiva/Lingayata scriptures do not consider Lingāyatism to be more allied to Shaktism; if at all any, it is considered closer to Shaivism.

The Founder of Lingāyatism

'The rise of the Lingayat Religion and its founder'

The eleventh chapter is titled 'The rise of the Lingayat Religion and its founder'. Professor Sakhare states that determining the time that Lingāyatism was founded, and the Prophet who founded it, is a very intricate problem, and that certain things have been taken for granted which have confounded the intricacy. The things taken for granted are based on some hollow traditions handed down from generation to generation so that they have become a kind of gospel truths. Tradition is often fictitious and baseless; it is necessary to determine the truth historically.

Traditionally it has been handed down that Veerashaivism was founded by the five great prophets (Pañchāchāryas) who rose out of five Sthavara-Linga installations (stationary Linga installations in temples) in different yugas (ages/eons): Revanaradhya or Revanasiddha of Kollipaki in Balehalli or Balehonnur of Mysore State (present day Karnataka State); Marularadhya or Marulasiddha of Ujjani in Ballari District of

Karnataka; Ekoramaradhya of Himavat Kedara (in the Himalayas); Panditaradhya of Shrishaila Mallikarjuna in present day Andhra region; and Vishvaradhya of Kashi (Benares).

Professor Sakhare examines the evidence found in the literature, and vehemently argues in a prosecutorial way. If only he had applied this type of evaluation to the clues that were in front of him about the fallacy of the theory of the Aryan invasion of India, what a great book this would have been. He critically analyzes what he finds in the existing Veerashaiva literature and tries to establish the 12th century CE to be the time-period when Lingāyatism was founded, and that Basava was the founder of Lingāyatism.

Professor Sakhare gives two Sanskrit passages without English translation, taken from two Āgamas, namely Suprabodhagama and Svayambhuvagama. He says that the first mentioned Āgama professes to trace the origin of the Acharyas to the five faces of Parama-Shiva, and the other Āgama tells the origin of the Acharyas to have risen out of the five Sthavara-Linga installations as mentioned before. He states that the two Āgamas differ and contradict, unless the five Sthavara-Linga installations represent the five faces of Shiva. He states that he wants to find out from the available data whether and how far this is the truth.

Siddhanta Shikhāmaṇi issue

Professor Sakhare continues: The first and a very authoritative work in Sanskrit on Veerashaivism is *Siddhanta Shikhāmaṇi*. This is the first book because it refers to Āgamas, and because all other Sanskrit Veerashaiva books refer to it.

It is to be pointed out to the readers, here, that Professor Sakhare demolishes everything which is in Siddhanta Shikhāmaṇi except the part where Shatsthala is elaborately explained in 101 sthalas.

As the readers may very well know that Siddhanta Shikhāmaṇi (11) has been composed in Sanskrit as a dialog between Shri Renuka, a Pramatha (first Lord) sent by Shiva to profess the Shiva-advaita lore on earth, and the well-known sage Agastya of the Vedic period who has contributed to the Rigveda hymns. Shri Renuka is said to have arisen out of the Sthavara-Linga at Kollipaki.

On page 235 of his book, Professor Sakhare states that the attempts of the author of Siddhanta Shikhāmaṇi at making Renuka or Revanasiddha or Revanaradhya as the founder of the religion are quite ill–disguised and unsuccessful, because the Renuka of the book is none other than the author himself.

The author of Siddhanta Shikhāmaṇi is stated to be Shivayogi Shivacharya, and the Sanskrit running commentary called Tattvapradipika that is included there is by Maritoṇṭadārya of the seventeenth century CE (11). The first prefatory note referred to below is the introductory note by the commentator. **The dispute is about who the author Shivayogi Shivacharya is, and when the Siddhanta Shikhāmaṇi was composed.**

In the first chapter of Siddhanta Shikhāmaṇi (11), after obeisance to Shiva, the author Shri Shivayogi Shivacharya gives an account of his heritage. He is the fourth in the lineage of four Acharyas. The first one in the lineage is described as Achara Siddha who was well known as Shivayogin, who was foremost among the Shaiva saints, who was the great ocean of Shiva knowledge, and whose speech was pure in the form of devotion towards Shiva. The second one is a Shivayogi by name Muddadeva who was known as such because of his giving delight to all beings and because of his granting enlightenment to those who surrendered to him. The third in line is named Siddhanatha who has been described as one with a calm temperament, of pure mind, an authority of Shiva doctrine, and the one whom the teachers praised as the crest-jewel of the Veerashaivas. From that Acharya arose the fourth in the lineage by name Shivayogin.

Siddhanta Shikhāmaṇi text itself does not state when it was composed. Tattvapradipika, the running commentary that is included there by Maritoṇṭadārya also does not state when Siddhanta Shikhāmaṇi was composed. The editor of the referenced Siddhanta Shikhāmaṇi (11) Dr. Sivakumara Swamy, in the introductory part of the book discusses this issue and puts forward his evidence. Some of it is as follows:

- Basavanna has quoted the Sanskrit stanza IX.11 of Siddhanta Shikhāmaṇi in his vachana. This Sanskrit quotation is in vachana number 506 of the referenced Ganaka Vachana Samputa (12).

- Chennabasavanna also quotes the Sanskrit stanza XI.55 of Siddhanta Shikhāmaṇi in his vachana. This Sanskrit quotation from Siddhanta Shikhāmaṇi is in vachana number 1732 of the referenced Ganaka Vachana Samputa (12).

- In addition, Chennabasavanna quotes three stanzas X.47 through X.49 from Siddhanta Shikhāmaṇi in his vachana. This Sanskrit insert of three stanzas from Siddhanta Shikhāmaṇi is in vachana number 1555 of the referenced Ganaka Vachana Samputa (12).

- Chennabasavanna acknowledges the existence of the one-hundred-one sthalas in his vachana. The vachana number 1336 in reference 12 has this acknowledgement *"...ನಮ್ಮ ಆಧ್ಯರ ವಚನ ನೂರೊಂದು ಸ್ಥಲ (namma aadhyara vachana nurondu sthala) ..."*

- Chennabasavanna has listed all the fifty-seven Linga-sthalas from Siddhanta Shikhāmaṇi in his vachana. The number and the order in which they are mentioned in the vachana are the same as in Siddhanta Shikhāmaṇi. [There are forty-four Anga-sthalas and fifty-seven Linga sthalas in Siddhanta Shikhāmaṇi to make the total of 101 sthalas.] This list of the Linga-sthalas is in vachana number 849 in reference 12. However, in this reference the vachana ends abruptly (incomplete) after listing 45 Linga-sthalas.

- Allama Prabhudeva also acknowledges the existence of the one-hundred-one sthalas. This acknowledgement *"...ನೂರೊಂದು ಸ್ಥಲದ (nurondu sthalada) ..."* is in vachana number 799 in the referenced Ganaka Vachana Samputa (12).

- Allama Prabhudeva also lists all the fifty-seven Linga-sthalas from Siddhanta Shikhāmaṇi in one of his vachanas. The number and the order in which they are mentioned are the same. This list of Linga-sthalas is in vachana number 788 in the referenced Ganaka Vachana Samputa (12). This vachana ends abruptly (incomplete) at the website after listing only 39 sthalas.

The above quotations of Siddhanta Shikhāmaṇi in the vachanas of Basavanna, Chennabasavanna, and Allama Prabhudeva **seem to be sufficient to confirm that Siddhanta Shikhāmaṇi was composed prior to the 12th century.** In this regard, the editor Dr. Sivakumara Swamy states "It can be safely decided that the doctrine of 101 Sthalas was already known to the Sharanas of 12th century CE.

Further, the editor of the referenced Siddhanta Shikhāmaṇi (11) refutes Dasgupta's misconception that Siddhanta Shikhāmaṇi itself refers to Basava. Shri Dasgupta quotes the introductory comment for the Siddhanta Shikhāmaṇi stanza IX.36, and the stanza also in his book (13). The editor Dr. Sivakumara Swamy points out the misconception: 'This preamble belongs to the Sanskrit commentary on Siddhanta Shikhāmaṇi, not to the text of Siddhanta Shikhāmaṇi. What is found in the commentary cannot be attributed to the original text.'

The editor Dr. Sivakumara Swamy further discusses as to when before the 12th century was Siddhanta Shikhāmaṇi composed. He notes that it is after the 8th century Advaita Philosophy of Shankaracharya. Then after further discussion he puts **the date to be between the 8th and 10th centuries.**

- **Based on the above information**, it is certain that Siddhanta Shikhāmaṇi was composed prior to the 12th century, and therefore, **the question as to whether the first in the lineage described above is the great Shivayogi Siddharāma of Sonnalige, the contemporary of Allama**

Prabhudeva and other Sharanas of the 12th century, becomes mute.

But Professor Sakhare attacks the author's identity as given in the Siddhanta Shikhāmaṇi itself and tries to find when the author lived and composed the book.

In the first prefatory note at the beginning of the work, he continues, it is stated that the author belongs to the order of the Acharyas of the name of Siddharama who was born to his parents by the favor of Revanasiddha who, first known as Renuka, taught the principles of Veerashaivism to the pot-born sage Agastya after the Kali age etc. This information tallies with the Puranic account that Siddharama of Sonnalige (modern Sholapur) was born to his parents by the blessing of Revanaradhya or Revanasiddha. Hence the Siddharama referred to in the book as first in lineage is the Siddharama of the Puranas. The great Shivayogi Siddharama of Sonnalige was the disciple of Allama Prabhu, and he went with Allama Prabhu to Basava-Kalyana to interact with Basavanna and other Sharanas. So, the author was the fourth descendent of Siddharama and therefore was of the post-

Basava period. As the author was said to be fourth in the lineage, Professor Sakhare states that the author must have lived about the middle of the 13th century CE.

Professor Sakhare is now faced with the dilemma of how to explain the paradox. First, he stated that the author of Siddhanta Shikhamani was none other than Renuka or Revanasiddha himself. Then he stated that Revanasiddha who was first named Revana blessed the parents to whom Shivayogi Siddharama was born. But the author is said to be fourth in the lineage, the first being Siddharama. If that is the case, the Revanasiddha who blessed the parents of Siddharama cannot be the author himself. Professor Sakhare blames the author of Siddhanta Shikhamani for 'creating this absurdity', and states that Revanasiddha who blessed the parents of Siddharama must be a person different from the Revanasiddha with whom the author identifies himself; this is exactly the position and cannot be anything else.

Professor Sakhare then gives this lineage. The elder Revanasiddha who blessed the parents of the great Shivayogi Siddharama was a senior contemporary of Basavanna. He had a son by the name Rudramuni who had a disciple named Muktimuni. Muktimuni in turn had a disciple called Digambar Muktimuni who founded a Matha at Rambhapuri. The Kannada translation of Rambhapuri is Balehalli which is the present Balehonnur. The Balehonnur Matha is the pontifical seat of Revanaradhya. The founder Digambara Muktimuni named the Matha after Revanasiddha the father of Rudramuni, out of respect for him. But by the time that Shivayogi came to succeed to the line of Siddharameshvara, this Matha must have attained eminence and earned the reputation in the cause of the religion. Shivayogi then must have thought fit to father the religion upon Revanasiddheshvara after whom the Matha was named.

Professor Sakhare continues. Shivayogi, in his eagerness to make the religion very ancient, has attempted to make Revanasiddha an avatara (incarnation) of Renuka, and has taken him back to the times of Vibhishana (he was the younger brother of Ravana of Sri-Lanka of the Ramayana epic). But he has failed so badly in his attempts. Anyhow, the example furnished by Shivayogi was imitated by his successors. They conveniently started the tradition of the remaining Aradhyas also being the founders of religion, as their Mathas came to be founded in due course and attained reputation in the cause of the religion. This theory of five Acharyas being the founder of the religion is a myth; it is not true. Siddhanta Shikhāmaṇi is the only book in which Revanasiddha has been stated to have preached and promulgated the religion. In no other Sanskrit book, he has been described as the founder of the religion. Also, there is no mention of the other four Acharyas being the founders.

Other considerations

Professor Sakhare continues: Apart from the above historical information, there are two other considerations. One is that Kashmir Shivādvaita did not exist before 9th century CE, and Shaktivishishṭādvaita is based on the Kashmir Shivādvaita philosophy. The other is that there is no evidence of the existence of Ashṭāvaraṇa, Shatsthala, and Pañchāchāra before the 12th century CE (this is not correct).

Professor Sakhare states that there are clear and unmistakable references to the Ātma-vimarsha of Kashmir Shaivism in the Sanskrit treatises of Lingayat religion (Shivādvaitadarpana), and Shaktivishishṭādvaita is only the modified or improved name of Kashmir Shivādvaita; this establishes that Kashmir Shivādvaita is adopted as the basis of Lingayat religion; Vasu-Gupta, the founder of Kashmir philosophy has been proven to have lived in the ninth century CE; therefore, Shaktivishishṭādvaita cannot be early and ancient. Professor Sakhare making such statements does not prove anything pertinent. Whether the Sanskrit Veerashaiva treatises refer to Ātma-vimarsha of Kashmir Shaivism or not is not in conflict. He stacks everything on it, and states that it is Shaktivishishṭādvaita and that it is the philosophy of Lingayatas. There is no proof to make such a claim; it is not acceptable. Further discussion of this issue is in the next chapter under Philosophy.

Then Professor Sakhare goes on to the second consideration. He states that the eight components of Ashṭāvaraṇa existed before the 12th century CE, but not in the form in which they are meaningfully connected in the ritualism of Lingayat religion. So also, there is no evidence of Shatsthala philosophy existing before the time of Basava. Hence, he says, it is conclusive that there was no Lingāyatism before the 12th century CE.

Comments on Ashṭāvaraṇa: The question is not whether the components of Ashṭāvaraṇa existed before the 12th century or not, but it is about the use by Lingayatas. Professor Sakhare has clearly stated that the vachana literature of Basavanna and his contemporary philosophers of the 12th century is the basic scripture of Lingayatas. If that is the case, then what do the vachanas say about Ashṭāvaraṇa? It is to be pointed out to the readers that the term 'Ashṭāvaraṇa' does not come in any of the 1426 vachanas of Basavanna. Furthermore, the term 'Ashṭāvaraṇa' does not come in Shunya Sampadane (14) and does not come in Siddhanta Shikhāmaṇi (11). Guru, Linga, and Jangama are emphasized, Prasada is not the same as it is in Ashṭāvaraṇa; it is serenity. Padodaka is also not as it is in Ashṭāvaraṇa; it is bliss. Vibhuti, Rudraksha and mantra are not emphasized. Therefore, there is no ritualism involved.

Comments on the statement that there was no Lingāyatism before the 12th century CE: It is agreed that the term 'Lingāyatism' or equivalent does not come in any literature prior to the 12th century. But it is said that Veerashaivism existed prior to Basavanna's time, and that the present day Veerashaivism is from Basavanna and his contemporary philosophers. Shunya Sampadane (14), the main scripture of the Veerashaivas, itself in its fourth lesson entitled 'The Sampadane concerning the Grace bestowed by Basavanna upon Chennabasavanna', given on page 24 in Kannada and page 25 in English in volume II of the reference (14) states that Basaveshvara restored the practice of Veerashaivism which had been tarnished by the six Darshana systems and six Samaya creeds. The six Darshana systems are the six philosophical schools, namely, Samkhya, Yoga, Nyaya, Vaisheshika, Purva-Mimamsa, and Uttara-Mimamsa. The six creeds are the six Tantra creeds, namely, Shaiva, Shakta, Vaishnava, Ganapathy, Soura, and Kapalika. Based on this alone, it can be stated that Veerashaiva philosophy and practices existed prior to Basavanna's reformation of Veerashaivism, and Veerashaivism owes its present form to Basavanna. Further evidence that Veerashaivism existed prior to the 12th century CE is to come below in this book.

Āgama issue

Next, Professor Sakhare attacks the Agamas, particularly the Uttara-bhagas (latter parts) of the Shivāgamas. He states that much stress has been placed on the Agamas that contain the doctrines of the Veerashaivas. It is implied that the latter parts of the Agamas contain the doctrines of Veerashaivism. He states that 'we have already seen how the Agamas have grown so bulky by continuous additions made to them even in the times after Basava'. Allama Prabhu, Basava, and Chennabasavanna come to be referred in them. Historically such additions are very late additions. *Anubhava-sūtra* is an important small Sanskrit book written by Mayideva who an admirer of Basava was. This book forms a part of Vatulottaragama as may be known from the colophons. Professor Sakhare here gives a list of eight items in Sanskrit only, without any English translation, and states that this is a clear instance of late inserts we have found so far. Thus, he states, it is very unreasonable to believe in the authority of the Agamas whose origin goes back to the time of the Āraṇyakas that all these existed then; hence the references to the Acharyas in them are late additions, pure and simple.

It is to be pointed out to the readers that, sure there are post-Basava additions to the latter parts of the Shivāgamas but does that necessarily mean that all the Veerashaiva doctrines in them are the post-Basava additions. Professor Sakhare implies that all the doctrines of the Veerashaivas in the Uttara-bhagas of the Shivāgamas are also later additions after the time of Basava. This is not the case (2).

The Acharyas

Then, Professor Sakhare praises the Acharyas: 'We have every respect and all reverence for the Acharyas. We adore, venerate, and worship them in deep gratitude for what they have done to the Lingayat religion and the Lingayat world by propagating and stabilizing the religion. They chose important centers in India from which to do the work in service of the religion and the creed. Their work is admirable, their exertions are praiseworthy, and they have made themselves immortal, not by founding the religion, but by propagating and stabilizing it'.

After that, Professor Sakhare takes the Acharyas one by one and tries to establish that they are not the founders of the Veerashaiva/Lingāyata religion. He then states that the so called Veerashaiva Acharyas are not the originators of the faith, because some of them are found to be contemporaries of Basava, and others even later than Basava. Basava and his colleagues do not mention the Acharyas in their Vachana literature (it is not the case; the Acharyas are mentioned in the vachanas, not by name, but as **'ಅಧ್ಯರು, ಪ್ರಮಥರು, ಪುರಾತನರು, ಮತ್ತು ಪುರಾತರು'** 'Aadyaru', 'Pramatharu', 'Puraatanaru', and 'Puraataru'). If the Acharyas had founded the religion before Basava, surely the Acharyas would have been mentioned there with reverence. Hence the Acharyas were not the originators of the Veerashaiva faith. Who then is the founder of the faith? Our emphatic answer is Basaveshvara. He writes.

Basavanna's Linga-diksha

Professor Sakhare on page 273 makes this terse statement: "there is nowhere any mention of Basava having got Linga-Diksha from anybody. He himself was responsible for his Linga-diksha. This is another way of saying that he and he alone started Linga-diksha on the cult of the Ishtalinga."

It is unfortunate that Professor Sakhare makes such dogmatic and derogatory statement. The term 'cult' means a religious veneration, but more commonly it means a religious group of people showing faddish devotion with exaggerated zeal or craze; the term cult is usually considered as derogatory. Furthermore, Professor Sakhare is using this term for Lingayatas whom he says belong to a distinct religion. Why he makes such a statement is not clear.

Although the part of his statement saying 'cult of the Ishtalinga' is somewhat derogatory, another point is to be made here. Professor Sakhare states that there is nowhere any mention of Basava having got Linga-diksha from anybody. This is not correct. The question is not whether Basavanna had Linga-diksha or not; Professor Sakhare categorically states that it is nowhere mentioned.

The referenced Shunya Sampadane (14), on page 4 of volume II, states as follows: 'Accounts differ regarding the time and the place of the initiation of Basavanna. According to Singiraja (Singiraja Purana chapter V.54-61, pp. 67-68) it was performed by Jatavedamuni at Bagevadi soon after the birth of Basavanna. Bhimakavi (Basava Purana Ch. III.24-29, pp. 40-41) agrees with Singiraja regarding the time and place of the ceremony but says that it was Sangameshvara Himself who performed the rite. Furthermore, the editor of the referenced Siddhanta Shikhāmaṇi (11), states in its note section on page 378: Basavanna obtained his Veerashaiva Diksha from Shri Jataveda Muni (Sangameshvara Swamiji) of Sarangmath at Kudala Sangama.

It is not clear why Professor Sakhare states that there is nowhere any mention of Basava having the initiation procedure. He refers to Singiraja Purana and Basava Purana in his book, and it is mentioned there according to the referenced Shunya Sampadane (14). But why does he make such a false claim?

Basavanna is the founder

Next, Professor Sakhare goes over a long list of reasons why he thinks that Basava is the founder of this religion.

Then he states that *Shivanubhavamantapa*, the glorious institution of Basava and his colleagues was the birthplace and the cradle of Veerashaivism. It was a religious institution originated by Basava and presided over by Allama Prabhu, a tremendously great spiritual personage.

After all his critical analysis he comes to the following conclusion:

Basava was the originator of the Veerashaiva faith in the 12th century CE. The first Veerashaiva Pontific Throne was that of Allama Prabhu. It was known as Shunyasimhasana; it was in Basava Kalyana. The five pontifical thrones of the above mentioned five Acharyas were established later (post-Basava) to propagate the Veerashaiva faith and to protect it against aggressors.

Philosophy and Practice

The twelfth chapter with the title 'Philosophy and Practice of the Lingayat Religion' is the longest chapter. It has 144 pages of text. Professor Sakhare, rightfully, opens the chapter stating that giving the philosophy and practice of the Lingayat religion is the most difficult task indeed. He also says:

"It is certain that we shall not be able to do justice to the subject. We profess our incompetence and inability to set forth the doctrines of the religion fully and properly, though we shall try to perform the task to the best of our ability, now that it has fallen to our lot".

It appears that when he states 'we' in the passage, it probably refers to just him alone. Professor Sakhare is very humble in respect of the enormity of the task ahead of him. That is indeed very nice of him. However, as can be seen from the following discussion, what he says as above, that it is certain that he shall not be able to do justice to the subject, and that he professes his incompetence and inability to set forth the Veerashaiva/Lingayata doctrines fully and properly, may become evident to the readers.

Professor Sakhare defines 'religion' as follows: 'A religion may be defined as a system of belief in the Superhuman Power, which governs the course of the universe and the human life in it and is entitled to some form of worship from the human beings for their attaining of eternal happiness'.

It is to be pointed out to the readers that 'religion' is difficult to define. It is said that a religion refers to a set of variously organized beliefs about the relationship between natural and supernatural aspects of reality, and about the role of humans in this relationship (Wikipedia.org).

Religion, Professor Sakhare says, has two parts, namely, philosophy and practice. Philosophy is the belief system concerning the relation of the universe and the individual to the Higher Power; it connotes a doctrine that explains all this along with the code of conduct for the practitioners of that religion. Practice of the religion is based on the philosophy of that religion; it is to attain the highest goal as ordained in that philosophical doctrine.

Professor Sakhare then states 'The Lingayat religion has both parts in it, distinct to itself, and can, therefore, claim to be a distinct religion'. The question then arises as to whether the philosophy and practice of Lingayatas is distinct enough to consider it as a separate religion. This question is further considered later in this book in the fourteenth chapter entitled 'The Status of Lingayat Religion'.

Philosophy

Right at the outset, Professor Sakhare states that the following sketch of philosophy is based chiefly on the Kashmir Shaiva literature, the Sanskrit books namely, Siddhanta Shikhāmaṇi, Shivadvaitamanjari and Shivadvaitadarpana, and the commentary on the book Siddhanta Shikhāmaṇi by Maritontadarya. As has been pointed out already to the readers, he makes this following statement on page xii under 'Argument':

"Though I am positively of the opinion that Vachana Shastra is the basic literature of the religion as its scriptures, I have based all my thesis with profuse quotations on Sanskrit books for the simple reason that my thesis centers round a Sanskrit work".

Again, on page 435 of his book under 'Lingayat religious literature and scriptures' he states after some discussion, '...*Thus the Vachana-Shastra of Basava and the Saints or Sharanas is the basic scripture...'*

The readers, therefore, should note that the philosophy discussed by Professor

Sakhare is not from the basic scripture which he himself states is the Vachana literature of the 12th century Sharanas.

Then Professor Sakhare starts with a statement 'The philosophy of Lingayat religion is monism and is called Shaktivishishṭādvaita'. On the first part of that statement where he states that the Lingayat philosophy is monism, there is no dispute. Monism philosophy is the oneness philosophy where everything is just one and there is no other; it is non-dualism called Advaitism. Monism is the philosophy of the Veerashaivas, and there is no problem with that part of the statement. The disagreement is on the second part which states that this Monism or Advaitism is of the nature of Shakti-vishishta. The discussion mainly centers on this part of the statement.

Professor Sakhare states that this term 'Shaktivishishṭādvaita' has been adopted from and improved upon Kashmir Shivādvaitism. He then discusses Kashmir Shivādvaita Philosophy, some of which is as follows.

Kashmir Shaivism Philosophy

On page 229 of Professor Sakhare's book in the tenth chapter titled 'Schools of

Shaivism', he gives the basics of the Kashmir School of Shaivism. Then on page 277 and onward he describes the Kashmir Shaivism Philosophy. Some of it is given here.

Spanda School of Kashmir Shaivism was founded by Vasu-Gupta in the 9th century CE. It is based on the scripture called 'Shiva-sutras'. It is said that Vasu-Gupta found Shiva-sutras lying under a huge stone, of which he had been appraised of by Lord Shiva in a dream, and that the Shiva-sutras summarize the teachings of the Agamas.

The earlier writers emphasized the Spanda aspect of Shiva, whereas the later writers emphasized the Pratyabhijna discipline. There is not much difference between these two disciplines.

Kashmir Shaivism considers Shiva to be the highest Reality that can be attained, and thus, it is referred to as Kashmir Shivādvaitism.

The only three attributes of Parabrahman, according to Vedanta, are *'sat'* meaning 'being' or eternal existence, *'chit'* meaning knowledge or consciousness or awareness, and *'Ānanda'* meaning infinite bliss. There are no other attributes; anything that is brought up is dismissed as not this, not this, not this. These three attributes of the Vedantic Parabrahman are the qualities of Parashiva expressed in terms of Shiva's Self-consciousness as *asmi, prakashe, and nandami,* meaning being, shining, and enjoying independently of anything else.

Shiva is the supreme entity. Shiva is the all-knowing, all-doing, all-sustaining, all-pervading, serene, indivisible and infinite. Shiva as the underlying Reality in everything is all transcending. Shiva's nature is primarily of twofold aspect – an immanent aspect in which Shiva pervades the universe, and a transcendental aspect in which Shiva is beyond all universal manifestations. Shiva is the origin and source of the universe and is Parabrahman.

Para-shiva's consciousness of self-luminosity *(Prakasha)* is also called *Chaitanya,* or simply *chit.* This Prakasha is said to be the most distinctive aspect of Shiva. Another term *'Vimarsha'* is used here to mean the power that may be called consciousness that results in will, knowledge, and action *(Iccha, Jnana, and Kriya).* The creation of the universe is said to be nothing but the ideal projection or manifestation within the Self by Shiva's Prakasha-Vimarsha. This power of Shiva is Shakti. The gender of the Sanskrit word Shiva is male, and that of Shakti is female; but neither Shiva nor Shakti is male, female or neuter; they may be addressed as He, She or It.

The creation of the universe is nothing but the ideal projection or manifestation within the Self by Shiva's Prakasha-vimarsha. The manifestation is real, not an illusion.

The Kashmir Shaiva Philosophy accepts the thirty-six principles (tattvas), but the concept seems to be somewhat different from that of the other Shaiva Philosophies.

Māyā pronounced as Maayaa is *Tirodhanashakti* and it begins to operate as the sixth principle (tattva). It is the power that accomplishes something that is impossible of accomplishment for any other agency. It becomes a limiting adjunct and gives rise to five limiting characteristics which become the next five principles. The Lord gets entangled with these limiting factors and becomes Jiva. It is the Maya tattva which breaks the unity of the Universal Self, and manifests diversity independently of any external helper or promoter. Thus, Maya, as a mode of *Svatantra-shakti,* causes phenomenal diversities.

The idea of moksha is that the individual soul must strive to be free from the three taints to attain recognition that it is Shiva. The discipline prescribed as the method of attaining moksha is called Pratyabhijnashastra. Pratyabhijna means the unbroken recognition of man's essential identity with Shiva. It is to be noted that it is a complete union to become one with Shiva; it is not living blissfully subservient to God.

For attaining moksha, Diksha (initiation ceremony) is as necessary as in the case of all the Shaiva schools.

Shakti is part and parcel of Shiva. It is one and the same, but the idea of separateness exists in the human mind only.

On page 280, Professor Sakhare states *"It is clear from this that Shiva and Shakti is one indivisible whole. The Lingayat philosophers give a special name 'Samarasya' to the intimate union. Samarasya means essentially one."*

Comparing to Lingayata Philosophy

Then on page 281, Professor Sakhare states "The philosophy of Lingāyatism is the same as the Kashmir Shivādvaita philosophy. But Kashmir philosophers have not given any specific name to their Advaitism, but the Lingayatas call it 'Shaktivishishṭādvaita' to give prominence to the wonder-working power of Shiva... Hence Shiva characterized and distinguished (vishishta) by His power or capacity to work, which is only a phase of His Prakasha in the form of Vimarsha. This is Shaktivishishṭādvaita. The Kashmir philosophers imply Shaktivishishṭādvaita of Shiva but do not express it in so many words. While the Lingayatas express it by naming their advaita 'Shaktivishishṭādvaita'. This is the first point of difference between the two schools, which is only a difference in terminology and an improvement in Lingayat philosophy".

The readers must analyze what Professor Sakhare states above.

First, Professor Sakhare states that there is no difference between the two philosophies. This is not correct. If the Kashmir Shaiva Philosophy and the Lingayata Philosophy are the same, then why are they two different religious faiths? Professor Sakhare himself gives the differences later here in this chapter. He solidifies the oneness philosophy of Lingayatas by stating that Lingayatas use the term 'Samarasya' which means, as he says, 'essential identity'. It is to be noted that no emphasis is placed on 'Shakti' in preference to 'Shiva' anywhere.

Second, he states that Kashmir philosophers have not given any special name to their Advaitism. This is not correct. The Kashmir Shaiva philosophy has always been called 'Shiva-advaita' philosophy - that is a type of Advaitism, different from the Advaitism of Shankaracharya which is referred to as, Professor Sakhare uses the term, 'Kevaladvaita' which means simple-advaita or mere-advaita or pure-advaita, and by default is simply called as 'Advaitism'. Shankaracharya's Advaitism is not called Shivādvaitism.

Third, he states that "Lingayatas" have given the special name Shaktivishishṭādvaita to their philosophy. Here, when he says "Lingayatas", it is not clear whom he calls Lingayatas. The Lingayatas are the followers of the philosophy and practices put forward in the vachanas by Basavanna and his contemporary Philosophers and Scholars of the 12th century CE. According to Professor Sakhare himself, the basic scripture of Lingayatas is the Vachana Shastra of Basavanna and the Sharanas. There is nothing in the vachana literature to suggest that it is Shaktivishishṭādvaita (15).

The fourth version of Shunya Sampadane (14) has put together 1,543 of these Vachanas in the proper scripture form, and it serves as the main scripture of the Veerashaivas. The Shunya Sampadane states that the philosophy of Veerashaivas is Shiva-advaita philosophy. The term 'Shaktivishishṭādvaita' does not appear anywhere in it. Shakti is mentioned in passing in the Shunya Sampadane; there is not much there about Shakti's prominence. Even under creation given on page 53 of volume I, it states "*...Nishkala Linga...by an impulse of its* *own spontaneous play and sport, putting forth the power of the glow of its consciousness, created within Self an infinity of macrocosms and myriads of microcosms..."* It does not emphasize Shakti or Shiva there at all; it specifies Nishkala Linga as the creator without the Shiva-Shakti divide; Shakti is Shiva, it is His consciousness. Not only that Shakti is not emphasized, but the emphasis also shifts from Shiva to Linga. Furthermore, the word Shakti comes in the five-volume books of Shunya Sampadane (14), according to the index pages at the end of the books, only 12 times (in seven vachanas). In comparison the word Shiva comes there more than 115 times, and the word Linga comes there more than 584 times.

The vachana literature and the Shunya Sampadane texts do not say that philosophy is Shaktivishishṭādvaita. Therefore, it does not make any sense when Professor Sakhare states that "Lingayatas" have given the name Shaktivishishṭādvaita for their philosophy. If he had stated that 'he thinks it is so', then it would have been a separate issue – that would have been his opinion – one should respect other's opinion whether one agrees with it or not.

Next, Professor Sakhare states that another reason why Samarasya (harmonious blending or essentially one) is emphasized is that Lingayat philosophers like the Kashmiris do not agree with and approve of 'Kevaladvaita' of Shankaracharya, the preacher of Māyā-vāda, the theory of illusion. Like the Kashmir philosophers, the Lingayatas hold that the creation is real and not an illusion. The readers very well know that this real creation is projected or manifested within the consciousness of Shiva and is not a separate part. Furthermore, Shankaracharya's advaita philosophy is simply referred to as 'The Advaitism', not Shivādvaitism. There is no doubt that the Kashmiris' and the Lingayatas' Advaitism is different from that of Shankaracharya's.

Then, on page 285, Professor Sakhare states that 'so far there is perfect agreement except in terminology between the schools of Kashmir and the Lingayatas'. Then he states that the difference lies in the explanation of the sixth principle (tattva) Māyā. According to Kashmir system, Maya is the Lord's power that accomplishes something that is impossible of accomplishment for any other agency. It is conceived as both the primary cause of all the limited manifestations (creation), and the power of obstruction. In the Lingayata system, Maya is not involved in the creation at all. Maya is that which hides the true nature of Anga and Linga. Under the influence of Maya, one continues to be ignorant without self-knowledge, and regards the world to be distinct from one's own self. [It is to be noted that this is a fundamental difference. In Lingayata Philosophy, Maya is not at all involved in creation. And as such, cannot be conceived as Shaktivishishṭādvaita.]

Siddhanta Shikhāmaṇi Philosophy

Then Professor Sakhare states that 'the mayavada of Shankaracharya is demolished and Shaktivishishṭādvaita established by Maritoṇṭadārya in his commentary on verse 39 of chapter V of Siddhanta Shikhāmaṇi'. He goes to Maritoṇṭadārya commentary on only one stanza out of 1367 stanzas in Siddhanta Shikhāmaṇi.

Before coming to Maritoṇṭadārya commentary, it is advisable to discuss the philosophy as given in Siddhanta Shikhāmaṇi itself. Siddhanta Shikhāmaṇi, composed in Sanskrit, is one of the scriptures of Veerashaivas. Further, Professor Sakhare states that he uses this book as one of the references to sketch this philosophy.

It is indeed notable that Professor Sakhare does not say much about the Philosophy portrayed in Siddhanta Shikhāmaṇi itself. He gives two half verses as reference from Siddhanta Shikhāmaṇi I.9 and II.2, in Sanskrit script only. These two verses are taken from obeisance to Shiva. English translation from reference (11) is as follows.

Obeisance to Parama-shakti (Supreme Shakti) by whom the Maheshvara becomes associated with name and form and who is of the nature of Maya. (stanza I.9, reference 11).

Obeisance to Maheshvara's Shakti, who is the pearl-oyster for the pearls in the form of all principles (tattvas) starting from Sadashiva and who is of the nature of Māyā-shakti. (stanza II.2. reference 11).

Then Professor Sakhare says that this Supreme Shakti is higher Maya, and that the lower Maya is explained by Maritoṇṭadārya in his commentary on verse 39 of chapter V of Siddhanta Shikhāmaṇi.

Siddhanta Shikhāmaṇi specifically states that the Philosophy of the Veerashaivas is 'Shiva-advaita' philosophy (Shivādvaitism). The term Shivādvaita comes many times in it, and there is no mention of Shaktivishishṭādvaita anywhere in it.

In the discussion of religious philosophy, the **creation** aspect weighs heavily as to what type of philosophy it is. The creation in the Veerashaiva Philosophical system mainly applies to the creation of the Universe. The soul is eternal as is the Absolute. The soul can be neither created nor destroyed. But, in the explanation of creation, how the Absolute becomes the souls is also explained.

Siddhanta Shikhāmaṇi gives the following information as to the creation of the universe and then how the Absolute Divine becomes the souls.

- The Parabrahman, also called Shiva, desiring to create the universe, assumed a form with exuberance of joy (stanza II.8). Then, His inherent Supreme Shakti of the nature of existence-intelligence-bliss, inseparable from Shiva in the creation of the entire world, on His desire, became one in keeping with the form (stanzas II.12-13). Shiva manifested himself as the universe through the Shakti form.

Parashiva-brahman is compared to the great ocean of pure intelligence, and the thirty-six principles (tattvas), not listed there, are said to have the appearance of bubbles of its waves (stanza I.3). These principles appear in sequence during creation. After this creation everything is still within Shiva. There is nothing outside – rather, there is not outside. The 36 principles from Shiva through Earth principle are modifications of Parashiva. The question then is what kind of modification. **Vivartavāda** is the argument supporting the apparent modification, whereas **Pariṇāmavāda** is the argument supporting the actual modification.

Siddhanta Shikhāmaṇi (11) itself seems to go against the Pariṇāmavāda and support the **Adhyasavada** (**Vivartavāda**) of Shankaracharya, as in its stanzas X.67, X.68, X.69, XVII.55, XVII.66, XVII.77, XIX.47, and XX.80.

As an example, stanza X.69 is given here: *Hence all this world which is consisting of the movable and the immovable and which is pervaded by Shiva, does not stand different from him, just as serpent-ness does not appear different from the rope.*

"A serpent or a rope" explanation had been put forward by Shankaracharya's Philosophy to explain that the world has not really been created and that the world appears real to only those who are under the spell of Maya (illusive power). A rope in partial darkness may appear to be a snake to an observer. At that moment the observer perceives the snake to be real. But when the light shines (when Maya's influence is removed), the doubt or misperception disappears, and one can see it is the rope not the snake. Of the two – rope and snake – only one is said to be real here.

The above example is an apparent modification supporting the Vivartavāda.

Stanza XVII.66 is another example, and it states *that the world apart from Shiva is false and Shiva is of the nature of consciousness.*

Stanza XIX.47 is yet another example: *The knowledge, here, is the state in which there is awareness of Brahman alone who is of the nature of the absolute blissful consciousness with the feeling that everything other than him is false.*

The above examples are consistent with Shankaracharya's Advaita Philosophy.

Shankaracharya's Advaita Philosophy is the one that is usually referred to as 'Advaitism'. This Advaita Philosophy is also referred to as 'The Absolute Monism'. According to this philosophy, Brahman is the only Reality, and everything other than Brahman can have no real existence and must be regarded as false.

Professor Siddhapparadhya in his Ph. D. recitation (16) writes: Siddhanta Shikhāmaṇi can be considered as the main authority for the Veerashaivas. But, by using the terms Avidya and Maye, Siddhanta Shikhāmaṇi may have veered towards Advaita-Vedanta. Further, he states that **it is more like Shankaracharya's advaita philosophy**. Some of his comments are as follows:

- Siddhanta Shikhāmaṇi has suggested to call Paramatman as Brahman and Linga.
- Siddhanta Shikhāmaṇi says Shivādvaita means Brahma-advaita. He quotes stanzas II.6 and II.8: "*That which is called differently as Shiva, Rudra, Mahadeva, Bhava and such, which is without a second, which cannot be pointed out, and which is no other than the ancient-most Parabrahman. Parabrahman is designated as Shiva".* He continues: 'There, Shivādvaita means Brahma-advaita. Shankaracharya's Vivartavāda is also Brahma-advaita. In addition to this, Appayya-Dikshita in Shivaadvaitanirnaya and other texts has explained in detail that Shivādvaita and Shankaracharya's Brahma-advaita are one and the same'.

Therefore, from the above discussion, it can be stated that the **Philosophy in Siddhanta Shikhāmaṇi is more like Shankaracharya's Advaita Philosophy.**

Discussion of Maritoṇṭadārya commentary

The verse V.39 of Siddhanta Shikhāmaṇi and Maritoṇṭadārya commentary on it, come in the first Sthala called Piṇḍasthala (not under creation). This verse 39 as translated into English (11) is as follows:

"Shakti of the nature of three guṇas, and who is ancient, adheres in the Brahman. It is by the disparity (of the guṇas) in her that the threefold distinction arose in it (Brahman)".

Professor Sakhare gives only part of Maritoṇṭadārya commentary in Sanskrit (Devanagari) and does not give translation into English. This is one of his main problems. He should have translated it into English and pointed out what exactly the commentary states.

Then as to this part of Maritoṇṭadārya commentary (11), it is about 4 pages in Sanskrit, and its English translation is about 7 pages. A brief but the main part of that commentary is given here.

The **commentary** starts with the word *"Brahmanishtha"* which is translated into English by the editor as: "Vimarsha-shakti is inherent in Parashivabrahman". The beginning of the Sanskrit commentary by Maritoṇṭadārya does not have the term 'Vimarsha-shakti' in it, but the stanza 39 itself has the term 'Shaktibrahmanishta'. Technically speaking, Brahmanishtha is the ishtha of Brahman.

Ishtha is the 'desire' or the 'wish'. Therefore, it is the desire or wish of Brahman. Brahmanishta is the will of Brahman, and Shakti is that will of Brahman.

Then the commentary continues. *'Samyoga'* which means 'conjugation between those that stay apart in different places' is not possible here because, there is no place outside Brahman (everything is one). Brahman being all pervasive, pervades without any break. (There is not outside for anything to stay apart.) Vimarsha-shakti resides in Shiva (Parashivabrahman) in a relation of identity which is of the nature of perfect harmony (Samarasya).

The term 'Sanatani' (literal meaning of Sanatani is 'the ancient one') is used here to mean 'eternal Shakti', the natural Vimarsha-shakti who is of the nature of harmony between knowledge and action. Such a Shakti exists in Shiva; otherwise, although Brahman is of the nature of luster (self-luminous), it would be without the knowledge of its own nature.

Shiva's natural supreme Shakti is heard to be of many forms such as Jnana-shakti,

Bala-shakti (Iccha-shakti), and Kriya-shakti, but not yet expressed. Because 'Chit and 'Ananda' are absolute, they are free from any disturbance. Shakti types are prone to disturbance due to their being related to objects. Hence, Vimarsha-shakti has the manifestation of unity and diversity and contains within self the entire universe of the movable and the immovable clasped in a relation of identity. This is according to the maxim pertaining to *'mayurandarasanyaya'* which means an argument that liquid contained in the egg has the subtle form of the prospective peacock (see comment later). This Vimarsha-shakti remains self-abiding as long as it is in a state of non-cognizance of division but assumes a form consisting of three guṇas in its state of cognizance of division.

In a portion of the Vimarsha-shakti, the part of action is free from the capacity to know, and the part of knowledge is free from the capacity to do. From the part of knowledge arises Vidya-shakti which is of the nature of 'sattva-guṇa'; from the part of action arises the power of 'rajoguna'. There is an essential unity between knowledge and action, yet by virtue of cognizance of division, there arises a notion of mutual negation; this notion itself is 'tamoguna'. This Vimarsha-shakti assumes a form consisting of three guṇas – sattva-guṇa, rajoguna, and tamasoguna. Then the disturbance of evenness among the three guṇas results in the formation of name, form, and action pertaining to three aspects – the enjoyed, the enjoyer, and the impeller – within Parama-Shiva who is of the nature of pure consciousness. Thus, by way of re-flashing, the Vimarsha-shakti assumes the form of Maya-shakti. It is through Maya-shakti that there is this accomplishment. Through this it is indicated that all this universe exists in the form of Vimarsha-shakti's cognizance of division. The One who is of the nature of pure consciousness, reveals, out of its own will, the entire world of objects which is hidden within itself and without any external material. This is in accordance with "What is non-existent cannot come into being". All this is accomplished through the will of Shiva.

If the beginning is made with the reason that it is due to relation with beginning-less '*Avidya*' (non-knowledge or ignorance), then Avidya-shakti would have to be associated with Brahman in an indescribable relation, which would be considered as co-existence with Brahman. Here, the beginning-less Avidya-shakti which is made up of three guṇas would be considered as the nature of superimposition on Brahman (*Adhyāsa*). Then due to the disturbance of balance among the guṇas, there is designation of three aspects in Brahman – the enjoyed, the enjoyer, and the impeller. Thus, Avidya-shakti would be considered as the material cause of the world on her assumption freely of a form consisting of parts in her aspect as Maya-shakti, as she is endowed with a capacity to accomplish what is impossible. In this case, Avidya-shakti is of the nature of defect and would render Brahman defective if the latter would be its substratum. If the world is regarded as a real object, then there would be no release from bondage, what is existent can never be negated. It is not tenable, because consciousness being uniform at both the extremes of beginning and end, it does not perform any action.

If an observer sees a shiny piece of conch-shell appearing as silver, there is an association with silver; the observer must have had seen silver before. Here, there is a superimposition of shiny piece of conch-shell on silver. In the same way in the case of Brahman on which Avidya-shakti appears, there is an association, hence the defect. It is like the acceptance of Avidya-shakti as a mirror outside Brahman which is the object of reflection. That is not possible, because there is no space outside Brahman, and existence of Avidya-shakti as a mirror outside Brahman is not acceptable.

In Brahman who is 'Nirguna' (without any guṇas or attributes), there cannot be Avidya; consciousness is without association. To avoid the contingency of the absence of consciousness in the case of Parabrahman, Vimarsha-shakti has been accepted in it as its very nature.

Further, it cannot be asked as to what the authority for the existence of Brahman is, because there is no authority apart from Brahman, and as such, it cannot be argued that Brahman is to be regarded as non-existent. This is because, Brahman is self-luminous by nature, and is always consciously felt through self-experience as 'I am Brahman'.

Discussion of the commentary: It is to be noted that, in this commentary, Maritoṇṭadārya does not mention, by name, either Shaktivishishṭādvaita or the Maya-vada of Shankaracharya. However, it seems that in the 6th and the 7th paragraphs of the 9-paragraph commentary given above, Maritoṇṭadārya is discussing Shankaracharya's philosophy, and saying that it is defective and not acceptable. These two paragraphs also refute the Shaktivishishṭādvaita philosophy by showing that there is no separate entity such as Shakti that is outside Shiva. It is inherent in Shiva; it is the nature of Shiva; it is in relation of identity with Shiva; it is not a superimposition on Shiva; it is not a co-existence; everything is one.

The explanation of Vimarsha-shakti in the first five paragraphs of the commentary given above seems to be what Professor Sakhare is referring to when he states that Maritoṇṭadārya explanation is Shaktivishishṭādvaita philosophy. It is to be noted that Maritoṇṭadārya does not use the term 'Shaktivishishṭa' or the term

'Shaktivishishtatva of Shiva' when he is explaining the verse 39 in chapter five of Siddhanta Shikhāmaṇi.

Shri Maritoṇṭadārya in his commentary on stanza I.6 of Siddhanta Shikhāmaṇi states that Shiva is always Shakti-vishishta. Importance is given to Shiva there. The stanza I.6 is the sixth stanza of obeisance in chapter one, it is as follows:

- *Obeisance to Shambhu with inherent Ambā, who takes many forms according to His (Shambhu's) free will, acts according to His free will, and creates the three worlds according to His free will.*

Maritoṇṭadārya commentary on this is as follows: According to Shruti (Rigveda II.33.9), Parashiva assumes divine auspicious forms according to his free will to favor his devotees. He moves freely according to his sweet will. He has created the three worlds by his own Iccha-shakti. He is the Lord of Parvati (Shakti), i.e., He is always Shaktivishista. To such Parashiva salutations are offered.

The Rigveda verse II.33.9 is as follows (7, 8): *With firm limbs, assuming many forms, the strong, the tawny, he shines with bright golden ornaments. The vigor is inseparable from* ***Rudra****, the supreme ruler and the lord of this world.*

It is to be emphasized here that the importance is given to Parashiva/Rudra.

However, Professor Sakhare rightfully points out one problem with the use of the term "*mayurandarasanyaya*" for explanation purposes in Maritoṇṭadārya commentary. It is an argument that the liquid contained in the egg holds the subtle hidden form of the prospective peacock with all its colored feathers and such. The liquid content of the egg is a material or a substance, and it is used there as a comparison to Vimarsha-shakti; and that liquid substance is said to have the prospective peacock which is compared to the manifestation of the whole world. This is not tenable, because Vimarsha-shakti is not a material, it is the power of Shiva, and it just represents the un-manifested condition of the universe within Shiva. There is no material content in Parashiva. The Vimarsha or the un-manifest universe in Shiva's consciousness should not be emphasized. Professor Sakhare states '*The illustration, therefore, is not to be stretched too far. Otherwise, the philosophy would be the philosophy of the Ramanuja's*

School of Vishishṭādvaita, if the un-manifest universe were to mean the subtle material condition'. Professor Sakhare's point is well taken; that is great.

As can be seen from the above discussion, both Siddhanta Shikhāmaṇi and Maritoṇṭadārya commentary on Siddhanta Shikhāmaṇi do not say anything about Shaktivishishṭādvaita philosophy.

Philosophy in other Sanskrit works

Next, Professor Sakhare states that both Sanskrit works, Shivadvaitadarpana and Shivadvaitamanjari, refute mayavada of Shankaracharya. There is no dispute that Lingayat philosophy is not mayavada of Shankaracharya. The question is whether these two Sanskrit works propose Shaktivishishṭādvaita philosophy. It appears that they do not. If they had, Professor Sakhare would have seized on it and stated so. Furthermore, both the titles have the term Shivādvaita in them, therefore, it can be said that they propound Shivādvaita philosophy as the philosophy of Lingayatas.

Then, on page 421 of his book, under the title 'The author of Lingadharanachandrika and his work', Professor Sakhare calls the author Nandikeshvara *'a bigoted Shaiva and a Veerashaiva'*. He then states: *"One remarkable thing to be noticed is that he never names the Advaita philosophy of Lingayatas as Shaktivishishṭādvaita but only as Vishishṭādvaita"*.

As can be seen from the above six works referred to by Professor Sakhare, namely, Vachana Shastras (that includes Shunya Sampadane), Siddhanta Shikhāmaṇi, Maritoṇṭadārya commentary on Siddhanta Shikhāmaṇi, Shivadvaitadarpana, Shivadvaitamanjari, and Lingadharanachandrika, there is no mentioning of Shaktivishishṭādvaita as the philosophy of Lingayatas. The philosophy mentioned there is the Shivādvaita philosophy.

Then Professor Sakhare states that evolution of the 36 principles (tattvas) as given in Shivadvaitamanjari is ideal or psychological. And then on page 290, he states that Lingayat philosophy of Maya is an improvement on the Kashmira theory.

Further, Professor Sakhare says, Lingayatas differ widely from the Kashmiris when it comes to the evolution of the relationship between the worshipper and the worshipped. Then he gives only the Lingayat version, and that too, as he states, based on Shivadvaitadarpana, Shivadvaitamanjari, and Anubhavasutra. It is briefly described below.

Sthala, Linga and Anga

Sthala, Linga and Anga are very special and technical in the Lingayat theology. Sthala, which ordinarily means place, means here, the ultimate substratum, or the abode of the universe. Sthala is not only the source and the abode of the universe, but also the place into which the universe loses itself at the time of dissolution (pralaya). Thus, Sthala means the ultimate itself which is the Brahman or Parashiva. And as expressed in Shivadvaitamanjari, this ultimate sthala is called Dhana-Linga. This Dhana-Linga, out of compassion for the Jīvas (souls) entangled with the world and subjected to all sorts of miseries and affections of worldly life, becomes the divinity to be worshipped – 'The Linga'. Lila (sport) of Parashiva is activated, and the vibratory motion of Perfect Egoity results in the Linga to be worshipped and the Anga the worshipper. After division, the Linga is as complete/infinite (*Pūrṇa*) as before. Linga is the highest Reality capable of being realized through devotional worship and meditation. Anga is a Jiva (soul) devoted to the worship of Linga. Any individual soul cannot be an Anga; only when Jiva becomes a worshipper of Linga, then it becomes an Anga.

Then worship and bhakti are explained. Bhakti in general means devotion. Feeling of devotion is always there in Anga. But the devotional feeling, or mental attitude of devotion must be associated with devotional activity either physical or mental. The activity, physical or mental, expressed by devotion is worship. Then it is said that bhakti is not just feeling of devotion, it is the worship of devotion.

Even though bhakti is the modification of Shiva's Shakti, bhakti is said to be superior to Shakti. This is because Shakti has the tendency towards keeping the Linga and Anga separate, whereas bhakti has the tendency towards unification. Shakti operates towards evolution or manifestation of the universe, but bhakti operates in a reverse order towards dissolution and unification. Shakti veils (hides) the true nature of Shiva, but bhakti attempts to remove the veil. Thus, the emphasis should be on bhakti, not on Shakti. Accordingly, Veerashaivas/Lingayatas emphasize Sad-bhakti (true-devotion) only. [This is another reason not to use the term Shaktivishishṭādvaita.]

Here, it is said that Linga puts the devotional feeling into Anga, so that Anga will have the ability to attain oneness with Linga.

Then, six-fold modifications of Linga as well as that of Anga are given. Linga becomes three, namely, Bhava-Linga, Prana-Linga, and Ishtalinga. Bhava-Linga then becomes twofold, namely, Maha-Linga and Prasada-Linga; Prana-Linga becomes Chara-Linga and Shivalinga; Ishtalinga becomes Guru-Linga and Achara-Linga. Similarly, Anga becomes three, namely, Yoganga, Bhoganga, and Tyaganga. Then Yoganga becomes Aikya and Sharana; Bhoganga becomes Pranalingi and Prasadi; Tyaganga becomes Maheshvara and Bhakta. Six Linga items and six Angas are related and are Shatsthala. The six Linga items are in the body of Anga, and Anga attains Samarasya through the sthalas of Shatsthala. Then it is said that Parashiva, the Parabrahman, is theologically Dhana-Linga, and that Dhana-Linga, Linga, Bhava-Linga and Maha-Linga are one and the same. It is to be pointed out to the readers that the vachana literature and Shunya Sampadane do not emphasize the six divisions of Linga and Anga; only three-fold divisions of Linga are asserted.

Principles (tattvas)

Professor Sakhare then states that creation of the phenomenal world is expressed and explained through the 36 principles (tattvas) identical with those of other Schools of Shaivism and Shaktism; they agree perfectly in sense and importance but differ in terminology; the difference in terminology is due to the special standpoint taken by the Lingayat philosophers.

At this juncture, it is to be pointed out that vachanas and Shunya Sampadane do not state that way at all (15).

Professor Sakhare's depiction is as follows:

First there is Transcendent Parashiva of the nature of Bliss itself. So long as Parashiva is the transcending Reality, Bliss and Intelligence as well as the one all-inclusive

Supreme experience of the Perfect, there is no need for a universal manifestation. This is Dhana-Linga, and technically it is also Maha-Linga.

The first manifestation is the manifestation of pure 'I', and there is no cognizance of 'am'. This Shivatattva of Shaivas is Prasada-Linga.

The second manifestation is the cognizance of 'I am'. This Shakti-tattva of Shaivas is Chara-Linga.

The third manifestation is the predominance of the will as 'I am this'. This Sadashiva-tattva of Shaivas is Shivalinga.

The fourth manifestation is marked by the rise into prominence of 'This' in 'This I am'. The power of knowledge predominates in it. This Ishvara-tattva of Shaivas is Guru-Linga.

The fifth manifestation is marked by the predominance of the power of action where a balance is reached without any stressing of either the subjective or the objective element, as expressed simply in 'I am this'. The universe is brought into existence. This Vidya-tattva or the Sadvidya-tattva of Shaivas is the Achara-Linga.

The body of Anga is a miniature universe, composed of the same five elements, namely, earth, water, fire, air, and sky. The presence of the Universal Self in the body is indicated by the six localities it occupies in the human body, and its activity exhibited in the five organs of knowledge and the five organs of action. Here, Professor Sakhare states that the philosophy of Brahman being confined into the human body and being in control of the sense organs is maintained by the Vedanta because it is said in Kena Upanishad. He then quotes Sanskrit verses of Kena Upanishad. The three verses I.1-2, and I.5, translated to English, given below are from reference 17. (It may be interesting to the readers that Kena Upanishad starts with the word 'Kena' which means 'by whom'):

'Who impels the mind to alight on its object? Enjoined by whom does the vital force proceed to function? At whose behest do men utter speech? What intelligence, indeed, directs the eyes and the ears?'

'It is the Atman, the Spirit, by whose power the ear hears, the eye sees, the tongue speaks, the mind understands and life functions. The wise man separates the Atman from the faculties, rises out of sense life and attains immortality.'

'That, which speech cannot reveal, but what reveals speech, know 'That' alone as Brahman and not this that people here worship.'

Professor Sakhare's quoting of the Upanishad, of course, is a pleasant surprise. He connects the philosophies of Vedanta and Lingayatas. The readers may very well know that the most important philosophical concepts of Veerashaivas are derived from Rigveda, Yajurveda and the Upanishads. [The readers may want to refer to reference 18 for details.]

Then, Professor Sakhare states on page 311, that the devotee gradually develops spiritual power and attains union with Universal Consciousness in the third ventricle in the cerebrum through the nerves of Optic Thalamus connected with Ajna-chakra. It is unfortunate that Professor Sakhare is saying that; it is not only wrong speculation but also not applicable to the Lingayatas. The Ajna-chakra is said to be the final and sixth stage for the union of Shiva descending from above, and Jiva ascending from below. It is to be pointed out here that it would have been better if Professor Sakhare had simply mentioned that the union occurs in the Ajna-chakra which is thought to be in the middle of the brain, instead of using the anatomical structures of the brain. It is well established in spiritual literature that the Ajna-chakra is in the middle of the brain at the level of the middle of the forehead where the third eye of Shiva is positioned. This Ajna-chakra has been visualized to be there by the ancient Rishis (seers) during their yogic meditation. The Ajna-chakra and the other chakras are not anatomical structures in the body, but they are often compared to them. This comparison to anatomical structures invariably leads to wrong matching. Professor Sakhare states that the Ajna-chakra is in the third ventricle of the cerebrum. This ventricle is a cavity filled with fluid in the brain and has no neural tissue (no neurons). The Ajna center is said to be the place where mental telepathy occurs – this cannot occur if there are no neurons there.

Another thing Professor Sakhare says is that the chakras are in the nerve centers or plexuses, specifically in the autonomic nervous system, and then gives diagrams of these autonomic nerve plexuses. This type of comparison is not applicable to spiritual visualization. He continues with such comparisons which are confusing and misleading. He speculates about the close connections between the organs of knowledge and action and connection with qualities of the elements. In this regard he talks about the touch sensors in the skin, the Pacinion bodies and the tactile corpuscles of Meisner, the special nerve connections between the eyes and the toes, and such. This is going out of his way to try to explain these things; it is inappropriate, not spiritual, and not acceptable.

Anyway, it is said that Lingayatas start with Linga and end with Linga, and therefore, they are Lingayatas, not merely because they wear Ishtalinga on their bodies.

In the above discussion, Professor Sakhare points out that there is some difference between the Kashmir and Lingayata philosophies. If that is the case, then, there may be a reason to use different terminologies for the two philosophies. Kashmir Shaiva philosophy has been called the Shivādvaita philosophy. Therefore, the Veerashaiva/Lingayata philosophy may need to be called something else. From the above discussion, it seems clear that it cannot be the Shaktivishishṭādvaita philosophy. The Advaita Philosophy of Veerashaivas/Lingayatas, can be simply called Linga-Advaitism (Lingaadvaitism). (15).

Summary of the discussion on Philosophy

The philosophy discussed by Professor Sakhare is not from the basic scripture which he himself states is the Vachana literature of the 12th century Sharanas.

Professor Sakhare states that the philosophy of Lingayat religion is monism and is called Shaktivishishṭādvaita. There is complete agreement that the Lingayat Philosophy is Monism. Monism philosophy is the oneness philosophy where everything is just one and there is nothing else. But there is disagreement that it is called Shaktivishishṭādvaita Philosophy.

Professor Sakhare states that this term 'Shaktivishishṭādvaita' has been adopted from and improved upon Kashmir Shivādvaitism. He states that in the terminology between the schools of Kashmir and the Lingayatas, the difference lies in the explanation of the sixth principle (tattva) Māyā. According to Kashmir system, Maya is the Lord's power that accomplishes something that is impossible of accomplishment for any other agency. It is conceived as both the primary cause of all the limited manifestations (creation), and the power of obstruction. In the Lingayata system, Maya is not involved in the creation at all. Maya is that which hides the true nature of Anga and Linga.

In the Creation, if the beginning is made with the reason that it is due to relation with beginning-less *'Avidya'* (non-knowledge or ignorance), then Avidya-shakti would have to be associated with Brahman in an indescribable relation, which would be considered as co-existence with Brahman. Avidya-shakti is of the nature of defect and would render Brahman defective if the latter would be its substratum.

In Brahman who is 'Nirguna' (without any guṇas or attributes), there cannot be Avidya; consciousness is without association. To avoid the contingency of the absence of consciousness in the case of Parabrahman, Vimarsha-shakti has been accepted in it as its very nature.

Shri Maritoṇṭadārya in his commentary on stanza I.6 of Siddhanta Shikhāmaṇi states that Shiva is always Shakti-vishishta. His commentary on this is that according to Shruti (Rigveda II.33.9), Parashiva assumes divine auspicious forms according to his free will to favor his devotees. It is to be emphasized here that the importance is given to Parashiva/Rudra in this Rigveda verse II.33.9.

Professor Sakhare then states that the creation of the phenomenal world is expressed and explained through the 36 principles (tattvas) identical with those of other Schools of Shaivism. It is to be pointed out that Vachanas and Shunya Sampadane do not state that way at all.

According to Professor Sakhare himself, the basic scripture of Lingayatas is the

Vachana literature of Basavanna and his contemporary Philosophers and Scholars of the 12th century CE. There is nothing in the vachana literature to suggest that it is Shaktivishishṭādvaita philosophy.

Practice

The practice of a religion is based on the Philosophy of that religion. In Veerashaivism, it is believed that the practice takes the individual souls back to the original source in the reverse order of creation and evolution of the individual.

Professor Sakhare states that the practice of the Lingayat religion is expressed very well by the definition of the word 'Veerashaiva' given in various treatises of the religion. The '*Dharmacharana*' is stated in the definition of Veerashaiva; it means acceptance/adoption and practice of the dharma (religious duties) of the Veerashaivas. He, then, briefly gives that information in Sanskrit from the treatises Shivadvaitadarpana, Veerashaivanandachandrika, and Veerashaivatkarshapradipika. Here again, it is to be pointed out that it is not taken from the vachanas and/or Shunya Sampadane which are the main scriptures of the Veerashaivas/Lingayatas.

Thus, he says, a Lingayata is one who practices Ashtavarana, Panchachara and

Shatsthala; of these, Shatsthala is all-comprehensive and includes in it everything that the religious practice expresses and lays down; the Panchachara and Ashtavarana are subsidiaries and auxiliaries to the Shatsthala; this is the very life and soul of the Lingayat spiritual discipline and religious practice.

Eight principles underlying the practice

Then, before giving the particulars of the practice, he goes over eight principles underlying the practice. These eight principles are well formulated and very apt. Professor Sakhare is to be commended for asserting the principles.

The first principle, he says, is that religion is as necessary for human beings as food is. A man without religion is the creature of circumstances.

The second principle is that it is a personal affair, the affair of the Jiva (soul). Every Jiva is the driver of the car of his own life so that he may avoid the ditches and pitfalls of ignorance and follow the safe route of the religion to ever enduring bliss, Moksha as it is called.

The third principle is very fundamental; it makes no distinction between sexes but gives equal opportunity to both sexes, male and female.

The fourth principle is the principle of universal brotherhood of man in matter of religion; keeps its doors open to all people without any distinction, irrespective of their caste or creed, rich or poor.

The fifth principle is that life in this world is in no way incongruous in the practice of the religion; it is not necessary for anyone to go to a forest for the sake of attaining Moksha; home and life at home do not clash and conflict in anyway with spiritual life.

The sixth principle is the simplicity and suitability of practice by means of simple and definite technique of Shatsthala; the Jīvas advance as far as they wish, up the spiritual ladder.

The seventh principle is ahimsa or non-injury; a religion is no religion that does not teach ahimsa, kindness and compassion.

The eighth principle is the unity of thought and action, or perfect concordance between knowing and doing; peace of mind or internal harmony is mainly because of one's satisfaction that one did as one felt.

Yoga

After discussing the above eight principles, Professor Sakhare states that the practice of the religion is Yoga. Different Yoga is requisitioned into service of the above principles to come up with the yogic technique of Shatsthala. This yogic technique of Shatsthala leads to essential unity of Linga and Anga.

Professor Sakhare continues: Of all the different forms of Yoga, Bhakti-yoga is the basis and foundation, because, without bhakti nothing is possible. The feeling of devotion (bhakti) prepares the mind and confirms the mental attitude of a devotee and enables the devotee to act sincerely in religious practice. Hence Lingayat philosophers give primacy to bhakti and Bhakti-yoga. All other forms of Yoga are complementary to Bhakti-yoga. Because, different individuals have different temperament, the Yoga philosophers have matched different forms of Yoga to the individuals according to their temperament –

Bhakti-yoga for the emotional, Karma-yoga for the action oriented, Raja-yoga for the mystic, and Jnana-yoga for the rational. All of this is included in Shatsthala.

Professor Sakhare is giving too much importance to Bhakti-yoga. This is not so according to the main scriptures namely Vachanas and Shunya Sampadane. The following is from Shunya Sampadane (14). The followers of Bhakti-yoga advocate the necessity of religious practice for the attainment of the Absolute. Bhakta of Bhakti-Yoga is a *paratantra,* that is, all one's words and deeds are governed by another, namely, God; the devout rely on God to help them in their spiritual discipline. The Absolute lies beyond the reach of diverse names, forms and functions. To claim that religious practice is indispensable for the realization of Parashiva is to distinguish between the means and the end. This shows a sense of duality which betrays a want of faith in the fact that God is inherent in the Consciousness.

Furthermore, bhakti denotes the concept of devotee and the Divine; it implies duality. To overcome this aspect of duality, Veerashaivas use the term 'Sad-bhakti'.

Veerashaiva *Sad-bhakti* has a special significance. It means right devotion, true devotion or real devotion. In Veerashaivism, the love of the enlightened individual is directed towards one's own Real Self. (Pages 357-358 of volume II of reference 14). According to the Veerashaiva Philosophy, devotee and the Divine are not two different entities, but two different names of the One Indivisible Reality (page 373 of volume II of reference 14). Furthermore, it is to be noted that Veerashaivas base their Yoga on the Raja-yoga. Shunya Sampadane (14) in its concluding remarks, includes this statement: 'This is the teaching of the attainment of the great Raja-yoga'.

Then on page 326, Professor Sakhare states that although the Veerashaivas have strong objection to the Vedic Yajnas inculcated in the Karma-Kanda of the Brahmanas, Kalpasutras, Grihyasutras, and such, they have special rites of their own. These rites are said to be intended to teach self-abandonment of all the so-called pleasurable things of the world, and to cultivate in the mind neighborly love and such. Thus, the religious rites of the Veerashaivas are said to be indispensable for spiritual culture and advancement. Then he states that 'these puritanical rites of the Lingayat religion are based on the Yogapada of the Divine Agamas; but this does not mean that other padas of the Agamas are neglected; on the contrary the Chara, Kriya, and Jnana padas are fully utilized and are made to sub-serve Shivayoga'. Then on page 328, he states 'in short, the practice of the Lingayat religion is Shivayoga that includes in it the elements of other forms of Yoga; it is based on the Yogapada of the Agamas'.

The statements made in the above paragraph by Professor Sakhare are to be analyzed. There is no dispute that the Veerashaivas strongly object to the rites and rituals inculcated by the Vedas. But it is to be noted that they also object to the rites and rituals inculcated by the Agamas. Shivāgamas deal with religious rights and practices pertaining to the Shaiva sect and are considered to form the main scripture of the Shaivas (14). Therefore, when Professor Sakhare says 'these puritanical rites of the Lingayat religion are based on the Yogapada of the Divine Agamas' he is not referring to anything pertinent to the Veerashaivas. Furthermore. When he says 'the practice of Lingayat religion is Shivayoga...' he is not talking about the Yoga of the Lingayatas/Veerashaivas (2).

Also, it is to be pointed out that Professor Sakhare is contradicting himself when he states that the rites of Lingayat religion are based on the Agamas. According to himself, all the Veerashaiva parts of the Agamas, are later additions after the 12 century CE. He is talking about the rites from the Shaiva doctrines, not the Veerashaiva doctrines.

Professor Sakhare, then, describes the religious practices, namely, Pañchāchāra, Ashṭāvaraṇa, and Shatsthala.

Pañchāchāra

Professor Sakhare states that the Pañchāchāra principles are intended to convey to the members of the community the principles of religion and religious conduct in general. Then he describes these five codes of conduct as follows:

Shivachara requires Lingayatas to believe that Shiva is the Parabrahma. He is not to worship any other deity. The devotee must maintain all through his life the faith and belief that Shiva is the only Godhead as the object of worship to the exclusion of other deities.

Lingachara is the worship of Shiva through Linga. The worship of Linga the gross or physical is the beginning of daily religious observances, prayers (readers should note that Veerashaivas do not pray – it is begging God for some favor) and contemplation. Linga is the Godhead of the Anga, the devotee, who should remain faithful to Linga and serve him faithfully, throughout his life, as faithfully as the devoted wife must serve her husband to the end of her life.

Sadachara requires a Lingayata to follow a profession and live strictly a moral and virtuous life. He should earn money by working in his profession for his livelihood and for supporting his family. He should utilize his savings and surplus for others in their needs. He should furnish his Guru with funds and feed the Jangamas. By sadachara the members are required to make no difference between one Lingayata and another but should take all to be as respectable and good as Shiva.

Bhrityachara is the devotee's attitude of complete humility towards Shiva and His forms of Linga. So also, he has to maintain the attitude of humility and respect to his Guru, Jangama, and Shiva-Sharanas. A Lingayata must adopt the attitude of service and modesty towards all Lingayatas as children and followers of the same God Shiva or Linga.

Ganachara is Lingayat's behavior towards the community. He should not tolerate scandal of the Godhead and ill-treatment of men and animals by others. As a member of the community, he must strive for its upliftment and development.

The above Pañchāchāra concept described by Professor Sakhare is from the Shivāgamas. The concept of Pañchāchāra according to Basavanna and his contemporary Philosophers is different from what is in the Shivāgamas. Importance of Guru, Linga, Jangama, Prasada, and Padodaka is emphasized repeatedly. Of all 1426 vachanas of Basavanna, only two vachanas have the term 'Pañchāchāra' (12). One vachana is the same one that is in Shunya Sampadane given below. It uses the term 'Pañchāchāra-sthala', and implies that it consists of Guru, Linga, Jangama, Padodaka and Prasada. The second one also implies that Pañchāchāra consists of Guru, Linga, Jangama, Padodaka, and Prasada.

Shunya Sampadane (14) does not give a clear explanation of the term Pañchāchāra. One place where the term 'Pañchāchāra' comes is in the first chapter where it says Prabhudeva was the teacher who established Guru, Linga, Jangama, Prasada, Padodaka, the five disciplines (*Pañchāchāra*). The term Pañchāchāra is mentioned there in the Kannada text, but not in the English translation. There is no other explanation there. It is implying that Pañchāchāra consists of Guru, Linga, Jangama, Padodaka and Prasada.

The term 'Pañchāchāra' comes in another place in Shunya Sampadane. It is in Basavanna's vachana. Basavanna is praising his nephew Chennabasavanna. Part of this vachana pertinent to Pañchāchāra is something like this:

'...Because, through ignorance of what Shivachara truly means, the world was perishing. Descending to this mortal world for other's sake, he firmly established the fivefold discipline (Pañchāchāra-sthala) consisting of Guru, Linga, Jangama, Padodaka and Prasada...'

The above vachana uses the term 'Pañchāchāra-sthala' that consists of Guru, Linga, Jangama, Padodaka and Prasada. It is not the Pañchāchāra of Shivāgamas.

Ashṭāvaraṇa

Professor Sakhare states that the Ashṭāvaraṇa items are the eight-fold shields or protective coverings of the devotee. They protect the Anga from the onslaughts of Maya on him and guide him safely to final beatitude after the life in the world. Professor Sakhare continues his detailed description of the eight shields namely Guru, Linga, Jangama, Prasada, Padodaka, Vibhuti, Rudraksha, and Mantra. As has been stated above the Ashṭāvaraṇa and its descriptions is from the Shivāgamas.

It is to be pointed out to the readers that the term 'Ashṭāvaraṇa' does not come in any of the 1426 vachanas of Basavanna (12). Furthermore, the term 'Ashṭāvaraṇa' does not come in Shunya Sampadane (14) and does not come in Siddhanta Shikhāmaṇi (11). Guru, Linga, and Jangama are emphasized, Prasada is not the same as it is in Ashṭāvaraṇa; it is serenity. Padodaka is also not as it is in Ashṭāvaraṇa; it is bliss. Vibhuti, Rudraksha and mantra are not emphasized. Therefore, there is no ritualism involved. Although Basavanna's vachanas, Shunya Sampadane, and Siddhanta Shikhāmaṇi give importance to some of the components, Ashṭāvaraṇa itself as an item is not given any prominence (2).

Shatsthala

Professor Sakhare starts by saying that the treatment and explanation of Shatsthala is a very difficult and arduous task – of course there is no dispute on this part of the statement. However, he states that Shatsthala is also called Shivayoga. Shivayoga, as he describes it, is practiced by the Shaivas, not by the Veerashaivas. It is to be noted that, here under Shatsthala, Professor Sakhare goes over an elaborate discussion of various subject matter that is not pertinent to the Veerashaivas/Lingayatas. This somewhat rambling discussion is in about 70 pages of his book. Some of that discussion is described briefly as follows. First, he discusses what Yoga means, and then he goes over different types of Yoga.

Yoga means 'union with' which implies that the human spirit is held to be separate from the Divine Spirit, and then the human spirit unites with the Divine Spirit. In its spiritual sense it means the method or process by which the individual spirit is merged in the Divine Spirit. In the case of the Veerashaivas (who are monists), Yoga is the process for regaining the temporarily lost identity of the Divine Spirit and the human spirit.

Professor Sakhare states that Yoga is both a science and an art and has been briefly treated first in the Shvetāshvatara Upanishad. It is indeed interesting to note that Professor Sakhare mentions the Upanishadic connection of the Veerashaiva practice. The readers may be interested to check this out in any of references 2, 19, and 20. Yoga as a science and art has been brought into prominence by the sage Patanjali.

Ashtanga-yoga of Patanjali, also known as Raja-yoga, aims at stilling the mind, so that the soul behind it is seen or the soul's liberation is attained. The quietude or complete stillness of the mind effects the destruction of the veil, and the soul becomes free from entanglements of matter and mind. Yoga is said to be an application of systematized knowledge of the unfolding of consciousness to the individual Self. Yoga is within reach of anyone and everyone.

Professor Sakhare then states that we must note briefly the nature and special character of the different forms of Yoga before proceeding further. Brief descriptions are given as follows:

Mantra-yoga: He states that he has already noted at some length the basic philosophy of Mantras and their use (under Ashṭāvaraṇa). Then he states that most of the famous Mantra-yoga Schools are out of vogue and have almost always been disregarded by Indian philosophy as such. Despite this statement, Professor Sakhare continues his elaborate discussion of mantra that is not acceptable to Lingayatas.

Laya-yoga: He states that Laya-yoga, also known as Kundalini-yoga, is of the Shakta School and its philosophy (Tantra Philosophy). Energy (Shakti) polarizes itself into two forms, namely, Prana and Kundalini. Prana is dynamic energy; it is the workforce of the body. Kundalini is a potential energy; it is located in the Muladhara chakra at the base of the spine. During this Yoga, Kundalini lying dormant at the base plexus is roused and made to ascend through the spinal column piercing through the other five chakras or plexuses above it during its ascent, and ultimately to attain union with the Highest Consciousness in the Sahasrāra at the top of the brain. This is Laya or merging of Jiva-Shakti with Shiva in the head. Laya-yoga is not applicable to the Lingayatas/Veerashaivas (2).

Hatha-yoga: Hatha-yoga which also belongs to the Tantra Philosophy, is said to differ from other forms of Yoga in respect of the emphasis placed on the physical side in the Yoga discipline. It is generally considered to be a method of forcing concentration by means of very hard physical exercises, penances, fasts and modifications of diverse kinds of food, sleep, etc. Hatha-yoga is also not applicable to Lingayatas/Veerashaivas (2).

Raja-yoga: Raja-yoga is generally identified with the *Yoga Shastra of Patanjali,* which is the first systematized form of Yoga both as a science and as an art. According to Patanjali, the ultimate end that is to be attained is complete isolation of Purusha from Prakriti. All the Vedanta Schools adopted this Yoga with certain variations in practice for the attainment of meeting the objectives specific for their Schools.

Raja-yoga of Patanjali prescribes a long course of eightfold steps; thus, it is called *Ashtanga-yoga.* The first step, *Yama,* makes it compulsory to observe faithfully the moral and social rules to enable the practitioner to adapt to the social surroundings. The second step, *Niyama,* consists of certain personal rules of conduct which are intended to turn away the mind of the practitioner from worldly attachments to facilitate ultimate success. The third step is *Asana* which is a course of posture-exercises. Fourth is *Pranayama* which is breath-control by means of which there is complete control and distribution of vital energy in the body. Fifth is *Pratyahara* where the practitioner practices withdrawal of the mind from the objects that attract the mind through sense organs. This steadying of the mind enables the practitioner to meditate unperturbed as in the sixth and seventh steps of *Dharana* and *Dhyana.* In *Dharana,* the practitioner focuses thoughts upon a particular object or inner Self. *Dhyana* is meditation proper where a continuous and steady focus results in an uninterrupted image in one's consciousness. The continuous meditation flows into the eighth stage of *Samadhi* where the image drops from consciousness and only the super-conscious state remains. When one meditates on a particular object, the Self is poured into the object which becomes the All. This kind of Samadhi is called *Savikalpa Samadhi* (with variation). When no object is used for meditation, the Self, free from all modifications reaches its own nature. This is *Nirvikalpa Samadhi* (without variation). When the lower self-consciousness vanishes and the super-consciousness manifests in the highest state of Samadhi, Perfection has been achieved.

Shivayoga: Shivayoga is a Yoga process of attaining 'at-one-ment' with Shiva the

Highest Reality. It consists of five elements, namely, *Shiva-jnana, Shiva-bhakti, Shiva-dhyana, Shiva-vrata, and Shivarcha or Shiva-puja.* Shiva-puja, the fifth element, is the primary element that includes in it the remaining four elements. Shiva-puja is the worship of Shiva performed life-long with devotion, one to three times a day. For Shiva-puja, the Shiva-jnana, the knowledge of Shiva, is the first necessity; the knowledge is given by the Guru, the preceptor. Shiva-bhakti is the devotion to Shiva; it is necessary to conduct the Shiva-worship. Shiva-dhyana is the meditation focused on Shiva; it is part of the worship of Shiva. Shiva-vrata is mainly bhasmavrata or Bhasma-dharana which is the application or smearing of the sacred ash during the Shiva-worship.

On page 362, Professor Sakhare states that five forms of Yoga are contained in Shivayoga, namely, Mantra-yoga, Kundalini or Laya-yoga, Bhakti-yoga, Karma-yoga, and Jnana-yoga. He also states that the readers might wonder why Raja-yoga is omitted; but the reason is simple, because there is practically no difference between Shivayoga and Raja-yoga except for minute distinctions.

This is not acceptable. Detailed rebuttal for this statement is not permissible here; please see reference 2 for explanation.

Professor Sakhare, on page 366, states "*We think it unnecessary to give details of Shiva-puja, as it is mostly modeled on Sthavara Linga-puja* (worship of stationary Linga in a temple)". The readers should note this statement, because the so called Shivayoga is applicable to the Shaivas, and not to the Veerashaivas. Despite his admittance that Shiva-puja, the primary element of Shivayoga, is not applicable to Lingayatas, he continues to describe and incorporate it into Shatsthala; this is not acceptable.

After the above discussion of various forms of Yoga, there is, in about 54 pages of text, an elaborate discussion which Professor Sakhare thinks is pertinent to Shatsthala. Shatsthala being the most important part of the practice of the Veerashaivas/Lingayatas, it can be stated that Professor Sakhare's narration is very disappointing, and may be described as somewhat bizarre, haphazard and confusing. He states that Shatsthala is the technique of Shivayoga and intermixes the elements of Shivayoga (Shiva-jnana, Shiva-bhakti, Shiva-dhyana, Shiva-vrata, and Shiva-puja) in order to explain the components of Shatsthala. Furthermore, the six stages of Shatsthala (Bhaktasthala, Maheshvarasthala, Prasadisthala, Pranalingisthala, Sharanasthala, and Aikyasthala) are not explained in a systematic fashion. It is an uncomfortable feeling to see the above five elements of Shivayoga mentioned and explained more often than the six stages of Shatsthala. Only some of the features of Professor Sakhare's discussions are given below. Most of it is not applicable to Lingayatas/Veerashaivas who follow the philosophy and practices put forward by Basavanna and his contemporaries of the 12th century CE.

The Shatsthala is based on the six places or spots in the human body that are the abodes of and that are occupied by the six Linga types, namely, Achara-Linga, Guru-Linga, Shivalinga, Chara-Linga (Jangama-Linga), Prasada-Linga, and Maha-Linga. These six places or spots are called Adharas, and they are Muladhara, Svadishthana, Manipura, Anahata, Vishuddhi, and Ajna. These Adharas are the energy centers and are also called lotuses or chakras. They are none other than the six chakras of the Shakta School. The only difference is that the Linga, the possessor of Shakti, is the wielder of Shakti, and is therefore, the occupant of the chakras and works there.

The practice of Yoga (Shatsthala) is not to proceed through any set of formal image-worship, and not to perform Yajna (sacrificial ceremonies); and it is not a prescribed form of chanting Mantras. It is by sincere devotion, aspiration, and surrender that the goal can be achieved. Complete change, down to the physical, is to be sought for the purification of the total being in its three planes that relate to Tyaganga and Ishtalinga, Bhoganga and Prana-Linga, and Yoganga and Bhava-Linga. It is said that the more purified the lower nature is, the easier is the descent of the higher nature. The purification of the lower nature and the manifestation of the higher nature (the Divine) progress side by side.

Shatsthala has devised the method of a gradual spiritual rise and development of Anga step by step. Ordinarily one does not learn to distinguish the three parts of one's being (Anga) that work with the three planes; these three are kind of lumped together and called mind, because it is through the mind that one perceives, sees, feels and understands. It is through Yoga that one becomes conscious of the great complexity of one's own nature and distinguishes the three different parts of one's total being. The three planes – material or physical, vital or mental, and intellectual or ideal – are said to be the three universes of the lower hemisphere, the human microcosm. The three parts of one's being, and the three planes are as follows.

The first part is the Tyaganga; it is the physical or the material part. Here, the earth and water elements predominate. The physical mind relates to various bodily organs, and subconsciously the physical mind governs much that has to do with the physical condition of the body. It is largely responsible for soundness of the body (healthiness of the body), or illnesses pertaining to the physical body. In this plane, the Divine presence in the form of Ishtalinga, first appears as the Light on the soul to be liberated.

The second part is the Bhoganga. It is the mental or the vital nature above the material or physical plane. Here, the fire and air elements predominate. The vital nature is life nature, and on the surface, it is narrow, ignorant and limited, full of obscure desires, passions, cravings, revolts, pleasures and pain, joy and grief, and exaltations and depressions. But the true vital being concealed behind this superficial nature, is vast, calm, strong, firm, immovable, without limitations, capable of all power, and all knowledge and all joy; it is the instrumental force for all divine realization. Through Yoga, as one becomes aware of this double nature, the exterior surface nature can be dealt with potently, and made free and perfect, and then one could manifest the internal nature, which is all divine, pure and perfect. In this vital or mental plane, there is the divine presence of Prana-Linga.

The third part is Yoganga. It is the intellectual or ideal plane, above the material/physical and the vital/mental planes. Here, the sky element and its source the Atman predominate. Although the second part the vital, and the third part the intellectual are quite separate forces, they are kind of mixed up on the surface of consciousness. Through Yoga, the vital must be carefully distinguished from the intellectual being which has to do with cognition and intelligence, ideas, mental thought, vision, will, and such. Once one distinguishes them as separate, the intellectual being within comes to the forefront. It observes, feels, knows, and reveals what is right. This is the highest plane of Yoganga connected with the Bhava-Linga, the intellectual or the ideal, the Divine immanence.

Yoga is a technique or a process of getting into consciousness where one is aware of one's own soul, one's own inner being, and the truth of existence of the total being. In the Yogic consciousness, one is not only aware of things, but also aware of the forces. One becomes aware of all this, not only in oneself, but also in the universe. There is a force, the power of the Divine, in the human microcosm coiled up in the base center or the base plexus, in what is called Achara-Linga in the Muladharachakra. This power of the Divine is waiting there to be awakened/activated during Yogic meditation.

In the practice of Yoga, the six energy centers (chakras/lotuses/sthanas/Adharas), have a general function and have their special powers and functions. The base center *Muladhara* governs the physical. The abdominal center *Svadishthana* governs the lower vital. These two centers are in the plane of Tyaganga in the domain of Ishtalinga and are occupied and worked by the two sub-forms of Ishtalinga – the Achara-Linga in the Muladhara, and Guru-Linga in the Svadishthana. Here, the force of the Divine is in a static condition, and the ego prevails on all that is concerned with the physical wellbeing.

The navel center *Manipura* governs the larger vital, and the heart center *Anahata* governs the emotional being. The two centers form the intermediate plane which is the mental or the vital plane. This is the plane of Bhoganga and is the domain of the Prana-Linga. The vital force of consciousness functions here. In Manipura the egotistic element is more prominent; it works in conjunction with the mind which predominates in the Anahata. The two centers are occupied by the two sub-forms of Prana-Linga - Shivalinga in the Manipura, and Chara-Linga in the Anahata. It is said that the real reformation and purification of the Anga begins here on this plane in the domain of Prana-Linga.

The neck or throat center *Vishuddhi* governs the expressive or the externalizing mind. The brain center at the level between the two eyebrows, the *Ajna,* governs the dynamic mind, will, vision, and mental formation. These two centers of the higher intellectual plane of Yoganga come under the domain of the Bhava-Linga. The two sub-forms of Bhava-Linga, namely, Prasada-Linga and Maha-Linga, occupy the Vishuddhi and Ajna centers respectively. Here the highest form of consciousness works as the true intelligent being and seeks the Universal Consciousness.

Then, on page 377, Professor Sakhare states that the nervous system, though complicated, is very important from the standpoint of mind and mental functioning. So, all the movements of the body are due to the strength of the nerves. Some bodily functions are wholly independent and automatic; functions of circulation, digestion, and such, are going on always ceaselessly in the body. This independent functioning is effected by the autonomous nervous system.

So far so good. Then he states that 'it is the sympathetic nervous system including the para-sympathetic nerves.' This statement is incorrect. The sympathetic and the para-sympathetic systems are two separate and distinct systems of the autonomic nervous system. Then he makes another mistake by stating that 'the respiratory system is part of this autonomous nervous system'. That is not correct also. The respiratory system is not a part of the autonomic nervous system or any other nervous system, it is one of the major systems of the body like the circulatory system. Professor Sakhare should have stayed away from making such wrong statements. It is confusing and not spiritual.

The six Adharas which the Linga types occupy and where the force of Divinity works, are the six chakras or plexuses. These plexuses are compared to and are considered as lotuses. The lotuses have petals and these petals, according to what Professor Sakhare states, are the main branches of the nerves shooting from the ganglia in different directions. Then he gives a list of anatomical structures that he says are the petals. Then he gives diagrammatic representations of these neuroanatomical plexuses and their branches/petals. This is all incorrect and not called for. All these energy centers (plexuses) are said to have been visualized by the ancient Rishis during their Yogic meditation. What is more absurd is that on page 384, he states that 'the mention of petals shooting from the plexuses is in no way imaginary but that they are veritable physiological parts of the nervous system'. This statement takes away any spirituality one might have had in the practice of Yoga.

Next, on page 388, Professor Sakhare states that 'the developmental features with which the six forms of Anga offer the objects to the six forms of Linga (here he uses the term 'deity' instead of Linga), are the six forms of Bhakti that correspond to the five gross elements (earth, water, fire, air, and sky), and the Atman that makes the sixth. Such is the teaching of Shatsthala for the practice of spiritual culture'.

Professor Sakhare continues. The Shatsthala includes the eightfold limbs (Ashtanga) of Patanjali-yoga. Some of these eight means of Yoga are to be followed by the devotee strictly, and some are to be adopted in their elementary form. The moral codes contained in *Yama* and *Niyama* are required to discipline emotions and strengthen the will. Both these come under *Bhaktasthala and* consist of some ethical principles relating to one's 'self', and also some relating to the interactions with other individuals in the community. By the earnest practice of the two types of moral conduct, the aspirant devotee acquires an excellent discipline of emotions, great moral courage, and unflinching will. The practice of Yama and Niyama also leads to renunciation of and detachment from the things of this world.

Some *Asanas* (posture-exercises) should be adopted as the devotee finds suitable. One is not required to follow and practice other Asanas that are intended for an extreme form of physical culture of the Hatha-yoga. Asanas are sustained postures of the body and are intended to be an aid to clear and collect thought. A suitable Asana is one which is steady and comfortable for the practitioner. The suitable Asana produces mental equilibrium. Padmasana (Lotus-position), or its simpler comfortable version of sitting cross-legged with a straight posture, is recommended.

Pranayama is to be practiced only in its elementary form. Its practice is necessary for steadying the mind, and for facilitating the withdrawal of senses from being tempted away by other objects – that is to facilitate Pratyahara. Pranayama is the regulation or control of breath. It is an attempt to lengthen the time required naturally for inhalation and exhalation, and for the retention of the breath in-between. It is said that the longer the retention of the breath the better, but it must be what is comfortable to the practitioner. Pranayama effects the physical wellbeing and soundness of the mind, and it is also helpful for meditation which is common to all forms of Yoga.

Pratyahara is the withdrawal of the mind from senses-objects so that the mind can be steadied and focused during the subsequent stages of Yoga. *Dharana* is the fixing of the mind on to one aspect or the inner Self. *Dhyana* is the continuous and ceaseless contemplation on the same. *Samadhi* is complete absorption of the mind into what was focused on during Dharana and Dhyana.

Professor Sakhare's statement that Shatsthala includes the eightfold Yoga of Patanjali (which is also called Raja-yoga), and also the description of that Yoga, are commendable, and are acceptable to the Veerashaivas. Shunya Sampadane (14), the main scripture of the Veerashaivas, in its concluding remarks, specifically states *'This is the treasury of the attainment of the great Raja-yoga'.*

Shatsthala stages are divided into two sections. Bhakta, Maheshvara, and Prasadi form the first division, and Pranalingi, Sharana, and Aikya form the second division. In the first worship-oriented division action element is predominant, and in the meditation-oriented second division knowledge element is predominant. Action and knowledge go hand in hand and ultimately belief prevails that action and knowledge are one and the same. Action and knowledge become indistinguishable from one another, and their essential identity becomes established along with the oneness of Anga and Linga.

Professor Sakhare states that in the Shatsthala the six-fold Bhakti is same for the development of any form of Yoga in all six stage that ultimately ends or ripens into Shivayoga with its fivefold factors; it is adopted for Shiva-puja which is the main factor of Shivayoga. Then he describes Shiva-yoga and its five factors as derived from the Agamas, and states that 'but here in Shatsthala, it is modified in light of Yogapada of Agamas, which form the main basis of the practice of Shatsthala'. This statement is not to be accepted, because none of the Yogapadas of the Uttara-bhaga of Shivāgamas that are pertinent to the Veerashaivas, is available to make such a statement (11). His interjecting of Shivayoga with its five elements pertinent to the Shaivas and saying that that is the same as Shatsthala of the Veerashaivas is not acceptable.

Next, Professor Sakhare states that 'now we proceed to explain the development of complimentary Yogas in order, which ultimately develop into Shivayoga'. Then he proceeds to describe the five Yogas, namely, Mantra-yoga, Laya-yoga, Karma-yoga, Bhakti-yoga, and Jnana-yoga. He had already described some of these Yogas at the beginning of the Shatsthala practice, but here he tries to integrate these five Yogas into the Shaiva's five Shivayoga elements and implying that that is part of Shatsthala. Again, this is not acceptable.

Near the end of this chapter, Professor Sakhare tries to summarize the practice of Shatsthala: The Shatsthala technique furnishes the scientific apparatus and procedure, which if followed carefully step by step, will enable the Anga to attain its objective. To the devotee, the details of the physical acts of worship are necessary only to strengthen the will. First, the worship of Linga is in its gross form, the worship of Ishtalinga. Next is the worship of Linga, both with form and without form. This is Prana-Linga and is an intermediate stage. Then there is worship of formless internal Linga that is the internal worship of Maha-Linga. Bhakti is the root of worship whether the worship is external or internal. Without this feeling of devotion, spiritual advancement is not possible. During Bhaktasthala, the Anga must learn and cultivate the proper sense of donation. Dana (donation) is giving of charity or making of gifts. Bhakta is to earn money by righteous means by following the rules of Yama and Niyama (of Ashtanga-yoga/Raja-yoga) and has to use it properly for the use of all. This mutual helpfulness of the individual members of the community is called Kāyaka (righteous ethical living).

Then he interjects – Mantra-japa and Dhyana are the main causes of spiritual development. They are the main items of Shiva-puja (worship of Shaivas in Shivayoga). In the second division of Shatsthala, Mantra-yoga and Laya-yoga may go hand in hand and might develop into either of their forms, but the end is the same. The result to be achieved by Shivayoga is Shiva-Samarasya or Shivasayujya. ShivaShakti (Kundalini) in the Muladhara is to be roused and made to ascend from the lower impure plane to the highest pure plane for perfect experience of Divine Consciousness. Mantra-yoga is one such means of rousing the ShivaShakti. The power is to be roused and developed for final emancipation; and Shatsthala is the technique for such rousing and developing power. The readers should note that he continues to interpose these things into Shatsthala; it is not acceptable at all.

At the end, Professor Sakhare states *"Our task is over. We are aware that our explanation is neither complete nor satisfactory, though we have tried our utmost to give the readers the meaning of Shivayoga and its technique Shatsthala".* He humbly admits that his explanation is neither complete nor satisfactory. Alas! It is unfortunate that he could not do a better job, particularly as it applies to this most important aspect of the practice of Lingayatas/Veerashaivas, the practice of Shatsthala.

Lingadharanachandrika

The main part of Professor Sakhare's work was the translation into English of the Sanskrit Lingadharanachandrika text. His original book consisted of an elaborate introduction, textual part of Lingadharanachandrika, translation of the text, notes on the text, and the appendices. The Karnataka University re-published only the introduction part of the original book as the 'History and Philosophy of Lingayat Religion'. The thirteenth chapter of this latter book is titled 'The author of Lingadharanachandrika and his work'. In this chapter, Professor Sakhare first comments on the author Nandikeshvara, and then comments on the commentator of Lingadharanachandrika. At the end of the chapter, he denounces the Swamis in general and Swami of Kashi-math, the Jangamvadi of Benares in particular.

Professor Sakhare starts by saying 'Liṅgadhāraṇa is the most prominent mark and feature of the Lingayat religion and denotes what it is. All philosophy and practice of the religion hangs on it'. Then, he gives the following information about the author Nandikeshvara and his work.

Author Nandikeshvara begins with the discussion about the internal investiture of Linga in the search of the Linga the Light (*Jyotir-Linga*) as it is the very basis of internal Linga worship. The author next proceeds to the external investiture of Linga and the external Linga worship. The author takes three texts from the Narayanopanishad, one from the Taittiriyopanishad, one from Shrirudra, and two from Rigveda, and explains them as enjoining the wearing of the Linga. The author seems to be well versed in Vedic, Puranic and Smriti literature, and the literature of the six schools of Indian Philosophy. During interpretation, addresses many principles and maxims of logic established by Purva-Mimamsa in support of his arguments. The author quotes profusely, especially from Puranas and Agamas, in support of the viewpoint taken during discussion. The author interprets the Vedic texts as laying down Linga-dharana with all pros and cons, refutes all the objections raised, implies that his explanation silences the carping faultfinders, and finally arrives at the conclusion. In this respect, the author is like the other commentators of philosophic literature. The author shows his skill in the art of reasoning correctly and expressing it in the textual form. Professor Sakhare states that in his opinion the author has performed the task admirably well.

Then as to the personal information about the author, Professor Sakhare states that only some meagre information could be obtained from two colophons. The colophon of the printed edition published at Benares states that the author was an authority on Vishishṭādvaita, and that he could establish in his disputations that Vishishṭādvaita is the essence of Veda, Vedanta, Upanishad, Purana and Mahabharata. The author never names the advaita philosophy of Lingayatas as Shaktivishishṭādvaita but only as Vishishṭādvaita. Professor Sakhare here states *"From this it is clear that he was a bigoted Shaiva and a Veerashaiva".* The second colophon from the manuscript B gives information that the author was a descendent of the family of one Panditaradhya. Professor Sakhare then states that it is likely that the author was a Veerashaiva Aradhya. As to the date of the author, Professor Sakhare states that it can be fixed approximately to be the 17th century CE, based on the prominent authors whom Nandikeshvara refers to in his work.

Here, a few things are to be pointed out to the readers. It is not clear why Professor Sakhare calls the author Nandikeshvara a 'bigoted Shaiva'. The dictionary meaning of the word 'bigot' is 'one intolerantly devoted to his own church or opinion', and bigot also means a fanatic, enthusiast or zealot. It is possible (mere speculation) that Professor Sakhare calls him a bigot for the following two reasons: One is that the author explains the Linga-dharana on the basis of the Vedic literature which is correct but the Professor does not want to admit it, and the other that the author does not state that the Lingayat philosophy is Shaktivishishṭādvaita philosophy which the Professor strongly believes in. The Vishishṭādvaita philosophy was originally put forward by the noted scholar Rāmānujāchārya of the 11th century CE. It is known as Vishishṭādvaitism. It is a qualified monism. It holds the view that there are three entities –

God, soul, and matter or Prakriti – which are steady factors, and these three form inseparable elements of one. God is the Supreme Ruler, the soul is the enjoyer, and matter is the enjoyed. All these three exist together both before the creation and after the creation. Creation is simply the manifestation in different forms by the will of God. If so, some state that, it can be categorized as traitism (belief in three realities), not Advaitism. Vishishtadvaitins believe that only Bhakti-yoga or Prapattimarga can lead to Moksha (salvation). They also believe that a person can attain Moksha only after the person's death. This Moksha means living blissfully in Vaikuntha (God Vishnu's abode), subservient to God Vishnu, not becoming one with the God. The readers should note that this Vishishṭādvaita philosophy is not the philosophy of Veerashaivas/Lingayatas.

Next, Professor Sakhare comments on the commentator of Lingadharanachandrika as follows. The work had been commented on by Pandit Mahamahopadhyaya Shivakumara of Benares. The commentator, although had profuse and elaborate commentary on the

Vedic text quoted by the author Nandikeshvara, his commentary on the principles of Lingayat religion was very brief. The Pandit had done his work well, but it was a sorry fact that the Pandit, though a Shiva-bhakta, did not know anything of the Lingayat or Veerashaiva religion. In many places his explanations were wrong. Here, Professor Sakhare gives a short line of Sanskrit text, and states that it is quite inaccurate, because the commentator takes *'daharopasana'* as *'pratikopasana* which is repudiated by Lingāyatism on account of the *'ahangrahopasana'* taught by it (Professor Sakhare interposes Sanskrit words in Devanagari script without translation or explanation; he should have explained it further). The commentator was paid for his commentary, and he did his duty accordingly as a hack-writer (hired writer). The commentator, therefore, did his work as a business, and not because he wanted to explain religious principles well. He lacked sympathy and real insight into the Lingayat religion that was required for this task. Professor Sakhare states that 'we do not and should not reasonably find fault with his commentary'.

Then Professor Sakhare makes this derogatory statement: "We may simply point out that the Swami of Kashi-math (Jangamvadi of Benares), a pontific seat of Vishvaradhya, one of the five Veerashaiva Acharyas, could find no competent Lingayat scholar to comment on the work. It shows the sad bankruptcy of Sanskrit Scholars among Lingayatas. The Swamis themselves, the heads of such sees and similar big influential mathas, should lack in requisite scholarship and insight into their own religion, for the promulgation and propagation of which they are intended, is a regrettable commentary on the present situation and the present of the Lingayat religion". Therefore, Professor Sakhare says, it was thought proper not to print the commentator's commentary along with the text, in his original book.

The Status of Lingayat Religion

The readers should note that, to give a clear picture of the forceful nature of Professor Sakhare's discussion in this fourteenth chapter, most of what he says has been taken word for word here. He starts by saying 'we have come to a knotty problem of determining the status of the Lingayat religion – whether it is a separate religion, or a sub-religion of the Hindu religion, or one of the Hindu religions.'

Professor Sakhare mentions what the consensus is: Lingayatas are generally considered to be a sect among the Hindus or a sub-sect of the Shaivas. Shaivism itself is generally considered a Vedic religion or a sub-religion of Hinduism. If that is the case, he says, it is not to be expected that Lingāyatism should have any recognition as a separate religion. The readers should note that the above general view that Lingāyatism is not a separate religion has prevailed, and it also seems to be the current view. Professor Sakhare, however, is not satisfied and he wants to show that Lingāyatism is a separate religion.

First, Professor Sakhare says that Lingayat religion has fallen into deep obscurity that it finds itself rather difficult to raise up from the obscurity and stand out in bold relief and shine in its glory that it may naturally claim to have of its own account intrinsic worth and merit, which he wants to boldly assert that it has.

Second, he says, even the Lingayatas themselves do not know what it is, much less, others.

Third, he says, the European scholars have neither studied nor cared to study the Lingayat religion and its literature as much as they ought to have done; they formed some superficial idea about the religion from hearsay and superficial study of a book or two, which would give no idea as to what it really is.

Then Professor Sakhare goes on to his blame game. The Lingayatas are themselves to blame for the obscurity into which the religion has sunk. Generally, the Swamis themselves, who are intended to be defenders and propagators of the faith, are so only in name in the sense that they have no insight into the inner meaning of the religion and its principles. They only repeat parrot-like the Ashṭāvaraṇa, the Pañchāchāra and the Shatsthala, particularly the Ashṭāvaraṇa components, and are not in a position even in the least to explain the fundamentals of the religion, when they are asked anything about the religion. In addition, there is such a sharp division and difference of opinion and of religious practices among the Lingayatas themselves of different parts of India that they are almost divided into different camps on account of different customs, manners, and views about themselves and their religion. There is little unanimity in religious rites and customs or real religious life among the Lingayatas. Swamis or ಅಯ್ಯನವರು Ayyanavaru, who have made a class of their own and call themselves Jangamas, though they are no better than birth-made pretentious ignoramuses, but like Brahmins of the Hindu fold, simply prey upon the ignorant masses. Professor Sakhare then exclaims *"Alas! What a lamentable state of affairs, what grievous parody of the religion, what a tragic condition into which the community has fallen!"*

Professor Sakhare continues. Lingayatas are the descendants of the Hindus. To determine the status of the Lingayat religion among the Hindus, it is necessary to know what the Hindu religion is. Hinduism is a common denomination or the highest common factor of all the Hindus of the Hindu communities of India. Generally, Hinduism is the religion as taught by the Vedas. But the Vedas do not teach any one common religious philosophy; they have a variety of philosophies and give rise to a variety of philosophical systems and practices. It is this variety that has been an object of pride for the Hindus. The Vedas, especially the Upanishads, are a literature of profound learning and thoughts, being the result of inner spiritual experience of great ancient sages. This vast Vedic literature is regarding the cosmic principle, the cosmic evolution, involution and life, the working of the universe and the individual souls, and advice given to the individual souls to follow a spiritual life to be free from the trammels of worldly life. From these teachings of the Upanishads, different schools of philosophy arose.

After saying all the above glorifying things about Hinduism, Professor Sakhare states that 'Hindu religion is said to be the religion of Varnashrama-dharma'. He latches on to this and believes that that is all there is to Hinduism. It becomes a main problem for his logic. The three components of the Varnashrama-dharma are, varnas (colors) forming the four castes, Ashramas the four stages of life, and dharma the duties assigned to the four castes and the four stages of life. He states that, it seems that at first the members of the community were classed as different castes in accordance with their mental and intellectual caliber and physical fitness for worldly duties; but gradually it came to be based on the birth alone. This made Varnashrama-dharma the most unjust social institution. The Veerashaivas have done away with it and have ushered in a new era of socio-religious life. Thus, the Veerashaiva community has been called *Ativarnashrami* a community above the Varnashrama-dharma.

Next, Professor Sakhare states that if Hinduism is Varnashrama-dharma, then it cannot include Lingāyatism in it as a sub-religion; the Lingayatas are Hindus in the sense that they are the descendants of the Hindus; but they are a different religious entity. In this respect they are like Jains who are also the descendants of Hindus, but they broke away from the Hindu religion and formed their own religion. But Jains differ from the Lingayatas in one respect – the Jains disavowed their allegiance to the Vedas, whereas Lingayatas seem to respect the Vedas. This respect for the Vedas of the Lingayatas has confounded their position and status in the community of Hindus. Professor Sakhare does not like the Lingayatas respecting the Vedas.

Next, Professor Sakhare states that he has established that Agama literature contains the culture of the Dravidians. Here, the readers should note that he is using the now defunct title 'Dravidians' to describe the culture of the ancient inhabitants of India; that statement is not acceptable nowadays; please see the discussion under Agamas. Then he makes a twisted argument as follows. The Vedic religion was the worship of natural forces and powers by performing Yajnas. The Agamic religion was the worship of images and deities. Then he says that, to avoid the cleavage between the followers of the Vedas and those of the Agamas, there seems that the two sections gradually came to be reconciled. The Agama followers began to respect the Vedas and adopted the Varnashrama-dharma. The followers of the Vedas adopted the agamic form of worshipping the deities and images. The religion practiced today by the Hindus is almost entirely based on the Agamas and has little or nothing to do with the Vedas. Hence, he says, image worship is the religion of the Hindus, if the religion can be so defined. Then without showing the proof that Hinduism is defined based on the image worship only, he states that, because the Lingayatas do not worship the images or idols, they are not Hindus. Then he says that Lingayatas are Hindus in only one respect as they worship the Hindu God Shiva. This twisted argument is not acceptable. There were no Aryans or Dravidians; everyone was the same ancient Indian. There was no Vedic-Agamic divide. That is how the Hindu Vedic culture evolved.

Furthermore, it should be pointed out to the readers that, contrary to what Professor Sakhare states above that the religion practiced today by the Hindus is almost entirely based on the Agamas, it is to be noted that Puranas are the ancient sources of almost all religious systems in India (11). The post-Vedic religious systems of Hinduism which represent the culmination of Vedic tradition in the worship of Shiva, Vishnu, Shakti, Surya, and Ganapati, are inspired and instituted by the Puranas. The history of Puranas can be traced back to Vedic and epic (Ramayana and Mahabharata) literature. The main aim of the Puranas was the popularization of Hindu-dharma. They were very widely used among the common people both in the original Sanskrit and in numerous vernacular versions and adaptations. The epics and the Puranas became the real scripture of the common people. They put the stamp of sectarianism. The people were devoted to some god or other, mainly Shiva or Vishnu. Puranas contain the chapters on the Varnas (castes) and Ashramas (stages of life), rites in accordance with the Vedic tradition, special ceremonies, Vratas (vows), and such (11). It seems that present-day Hinduism is based mainly on the epics and the Puranas, and not on the Agamas.

Next, Professor Sakhare states that after the (Lingayat) religion came to be formed (after 12th century CE in the post-Basava period), the new community altogether severed the connections with the Brahminic priesthood. They tried to maintain their position as being Ativarnashramis (those above the Varnashrama-dharma). In addition, they claimed to be *Aprakrita-Brahmanah* which means something like Super-Brahmin. He states that the topic of Aprakrita-Brahmanatva has been discussed in the Sanskrit treatise Veerashaivanandachandrika, and the explanation for it is as follows. The worship of Sthavara-Linga (stationary Linga in a temple) is *prakrita*; by doing such worship, one can achieve Mukti (salvation/liberation) only after three births. But the Jangama-Linga form of worship that the Veerashaivas perform is *Aprakrita*; it secures Mukti within the present birth alone. Thus, the Hindu Brahmin requires at least three life cycles to attain Mukti, whereas the Veerashaivas can attain Mukti in this very life while still alive; therefore the Veerashaivas are like Super-Brahmins. Then he says that the explanation of the practice of Ativarnashramadharma and Aprakrita-Brahmanatva by the Veerashaivas caused confusion and did not result in the independent status of the Veerashaivas. This confusion was further compounded when the support for the basic principles of the Veerashaivas was said to be from the Vedic and especially the Upanishadic literature.

Professor Sakhare blames the post-Basava Veerashaivas and the post-Basava Sanskrit literature of the Veerashaivas, and states that this confusion could have been avoided if it was maintained that they were an independent religious fold without giving such explanations. It is to be noted that these Veerashaiva scholars did not believe Lingāyatism to be a separate religion; there was no Vedic-Agamic divide, and there was no Aryan invasion and the Aryan-Dravidian divide that Professor Sakhare believes in. The basic principles of the Veerashaivas are indeed supported by the Vedic and particularly the Upanishadic literature (18).

Professor Sakhare continues. Although Jains and most of the Sikhs are descendants of the Hindus, the position of Jains and Sikhs is safe, as both have thrown off their allegiance to the Vedas and have maintained their position clearly by asserting the distinctness of creed, tenet and principles. 'If we boldly maintain that Lingāyatism is an independent religious entity, in spite of confusion and dubiousness caused to it by the trend of discussion noted above, we tread as a sure and safe ground regarding the status of Lingayatas and their religion'.

Then he says that 'when reduced to a tabular form it will be as follows' and gives a branching depiction that gives this information. He divides the Hindus into two main branches: the first one is the non-Vedic and non-Agamic branch that includes the Buddhists, the Jains, and the now extinct Charvakas; the second branch is the Vedic-Agamic that has two sub-branches - Varnashramic and non-Varnashramic; the Varnashramic sub-branch includes Shaivas, Vaishnavas, and Aryasamajists and others, the non-Varnashramic sub-branch is the Lingayatas.

Professor Sakhare concludes this chapter by stating "We avow that we have no quarrel with the Vedas or their religion. We do not in the least mean to entertain any separatist tendency. We discuss this question purely on principles as a matter of academic interest from the academic point of view. And we leave it to the readers to judge for themselves and see how far our conclusion is right".

It is to be pointed out to the readers that Professor Sakhare has not presented the evidence to prove beyond a reasonable doubt that Lingāyatism deserves to be a separate religion. Throughout this book, he has many false assumptions, and is not only dogmatic at times but also ambivalent at other times in his opinion and presentation.

Doctor S. Radhakrishnan wrote the 'Foreword' to Professor Sakhare's book. He was one of the scholars who wrote on the history of Indian Philosophy. He was a strong advocate of the Vedantic Advaita Philosophy, a slightly modified Advaita Philosophy of Shankaracharya. Doctor Radhakrishnan, later, after India's attainment of independence from the British, became the first Vice-President of Independent India and then the second President of India. Doctor Radhakrishnan in his Foreword states "*The author takes great pain to make out that the Lingayat faith is altogether independent of the Hindu religion which is primarily based on the authoritativeness of the Vedas and the Varnashrama-dharma. As the Lingayat religion accepts the authoritativeness of the Agamas and repudiates the distinctions of castes, it is said to be non-Hindu. I am afraid that this is taking a somewhat narrow view of the spirit of Hinduism".*

Lingayat religious literature

This chapter with the title 'Lingayat religious literature and scripture' is the fifteenth and the last chapter of the book. Professor Sakhare states that the confusion raised in the previous chapter as to whether Lingāyatism is a separate religion or not naturally leads to the question – was there no literature at the basis of the new religion that could have avoided such confusion? He then states that he is answering that question here in this chapter.

He starts by saying that it is already established that prophet Basava founded the Lingayat religion by giving a different shape to the then existing form of Shaiva religion. Basava turned Shaivism into Lingāyatism by far reaching and astounding changes that worked like a miracle and changed the socio-religious life of the Hindus of his times. Basava started Anubhava Mantapa for a thorough discussion of the principles. He was specially helped in this stupendous undertaking by his nephew Chennabasavanna, and by Allama Prabhu, the matchless Yogin who demonstrated to the world, his unfailing power of raising the practitioner to the heights of Yogic attainment. To popularize the new movement, the principles were preached and conveyed to the public in the language of the people, Kannada; it became the best means and medium of carrying conviction to them. The result was the Vachana literature. The members of Anubhava Mantapa, every day sent to the people, messages by means of Vachanas or sayings. The Vachanas are like Upanishads in their poetic fervor and profundity of meaning. Vachanas are short sentences, very telling, thrilling and soul-stirring, and unfailing in their effect. Thus, the Vachana-Shastra of Basava and the Saints or Sharanas is the basic scripture of the new religion.

As to the Agamas, Professor Sakhare states that the twenty-eight Shivāgamas are as much an authority to Lingāyatism as to Shaivas; but only the portions of Shivāgamas called Uttaragmas, the latter portion of the Shivāgamas, apply to the Veerashaivas or Lingayatas. The Uttara-vibhagas of Shivāgamas are said to be solely and profoundly inspired by the *Shivādvaita-*

Siddhanta philosophy, the teaching about subjective illumination.

Professor Sakhare continues. After the Lingayat religion came to be founded, treatises began to be written in Sanskrit in explanation of their religion and its fundamental principles. Siddhanta Shikhāmaṇi is the first such religious treatise in Sanskrit. Lingadharanachandrika is another one that came much later. These Sanskrit treatises have support from not only the Shivāgamas but also from the Vedic literature, specifically the Upanishads.

Another Sanskrit treatise *VedantasaraVeerashaivaChintamani* of Nanjannarya is all full of quotations from Vedas, Upanishads and Puranas besides those of Agamas. Professor Sakhare states 'writers of Sanskrit treatises, later than Shivayogi, the author of Siddhanta Shikhāmaṇi, lost sight of Vachana Shastra as the basis of the religion and as the basic religious scriptures; this was so because, they could not quote from the Vachana literature in their Sanskrit works'. He also makes the following statement: 'The writers of Sanskrit treatises also had to have recourse to write in Sanskrit because they were surrounded by the Brahminic Shaivas that adopted and followed Varnashrama-dharma and put queries in Sanskrit. The enthusiastic followers of the new religion had to meet their opponents on their own ground. They had to prove their viewpoint by quoting from Sanskrit literature and to explain the authorities quoted suitably to their own tenets. All this resulted in the confusion described just before; and Vachana literature came to be kept in the background'. It is to be pointed out to the readers that it is not certain whether this story like statement is true or not.

Next, Professor Sakhare states that it is no use taking for granted all things as they are in Sanskrit and Kannada literature from the historical point of view. Mahabharata and eighteen Puranas are ascribed to the authorship of Vyasa. At this juncture, he basically discusses the following. The core of the Mahabharata is called 'Jaya' which means victory. Jaya with its 8,800 verses is attributed to Veda Vyasa. 'Bharata' with 24,000 verses, containing the Jaya in its entirety, is said to have been recited by Vaisampayana who was one of Vyasa's chief disciples. Mahabharata is more than 100,000 verses and is the expanded version of Bharata. It is said to have been recited by Ugrasrava Sauti, a professional storyteller, to an assembly of Rishis. Jaya includes the well-known Bhagavad-Gita. Thus, technically speaking, Vyasa authored 'Jaya" including the 'Bhagavad-Gita', and not Mahabharata. Furthermore, it is stated that Vyasa's father Parashara wrote the original text of Vishnu Purana, and Vyasa authored the rest, and edited and presented all the 18 Puranas. It is also said that Vyasa's son Shuka was the narrator of Vyasa's major Purana called Shrimad Bhagavata. So many things seem to be ascribed to Vyasa. Veda Vyasa did not author the Puranas.

Professor Sakhare continues. He states that Puranas gave so much scope for later writers of different parts of India and different schools and sects to insert their own stories and statements in the Puranas. The result has been that there is no unanimity in the manuscripts of Puranas and other works of different parts of India regarding their contents. Lingayat authors also followed suit and wrote *PrabhuLingaLila* and *Basava-Purana* in the name of Vyasa.

To impart sanctity and authoritativeness to his work, the author of PrabhuLingaLila, SiddhaveeraShivayogi, inserts it into *Bhavishya-Purana* that is ascribed to Vyasa. Similarly, there is a funny story in Basava-Purana which is ascribed to Vyasa. Here, it is to be pointed out to the readers that although the Bhavishya-Purana is one of the eighteen Puranas mentioned above ascribing authorship to Vyasa, Basava-Purana is not one of those eighteen. The story is that Vyasa goes to Shiva in Kailasa and asks Shiva why Basava-Purana is more popular than all his other Puranas. Shiva then gets Basava-Purana weighed against all the other Puranas and shows to Vyasa that Basava-Purana is weightier than all the other Puranas put together. Professor Sakhare exclaims "how are we to believe all this?", and then says that we must take all this in the spirit that it was the enthusiasm of the admirers of Basava that caused such statements. How fitting!

Then Professor Sakhare appeals: "We, therefore, appeal to readers, at least to such as are Lingayatas, to work in the field of research for the truth of this religion and for gathering rich harvests of real truths and principles, and for effecting real reformation in the present sad state of religion; so that the religion and the community should feel re-animation and attain rejuvenation".

The readers should note that, only in this spirit which is called for by Professor Sakhare that this commentary on his book is written as a critical review. Furthermore, in response to Professor Sakhare's appeal, other books have been written and have been published; they are referenced here (2, 15, and 18). The interested readers may want to refer to them.

As has already been stated Lingayatas are the followers of the philosophy and the practices put forward by Basavanna and his contemporaries of the twelfth century of the Common Era. The twelfth century Philosophers did not give a specific name either to the new religious faith which has been referred to as Lingāyatism, or to its philosophy which is being called as Liṅgādvaitism. The philosophy and practices of this new religious faith have been documented in the vachanas.

In reference 15 the essence of the advaita philosophy has been extracted from the vachanas. The philosophy that has been brought out is the Linga-advaita Philosophy. It cannot be anything other than Liṅgādvaitism.

Also, it is to be pointed out to the readers that Professor Sakhare does not specifically mention Shunya Sampadane (14) in this chapter about the scriptures. It is possible that he includes it in the 'Vachana-Shastras of Basava and other Sharanas' which he calls as the basic scripture of the Veerashaivas/Lingayatas.

The last sentence in Professor Sakhare's book is *"We conclude our work with hearty prayers to God, the Universal Consciousness, nameless but named Shiva the Auspicious, and His consort Shakti, Vimarsha, also nameless but named Ambika, the Great Mother".*

It is astonishing to see this type of statement from Professor Sakhare for two main reasons:

First is that he uses the term 'prayers' as above in 'hearty prayers to God'. It should be noted that Veerashaivas do not pray. They worship and completely surrender. Use of the English word 'prayer' should be avoided. The word 'prayer' means an earnest request for something as in the act of petitioning God to grant a favor; it is kind of begging God to sanction something. It indicates duality – that the individual and God are two separate and independent entities – two Realities. Veerashaivas are monists and consider the worshipper and the worshipped to be one and the same. Professor Sakhare himself states clearly that the philosophy of the Lingayatas/Veerashaivas is Monism. Therefore, Veerashaivas do not pray.

Second is that he uses the term 'consort' as above in 'His consort Shakti'. The English word 'consort' means 'spouse', 'mate', or 'wife'. That implies that Shiva and Shakti are two different entities. Again, this implies duality. That is not acceptable to the Veerashaivas/Lingayatas.

It is unfortunate that Professor Sakhare, after all that he has stated in his book, and who is a firm believer in Monism/Advaitism of Lingayatas/Veerashaivas, ends his book with such a statement that is not acceptable to the

Lingayatas/Veerashaivas. Namah in 'Om Namah Shivaya' means obeisance. Obeisance is bowing down to show respect, or submission. He could have just said *Om Namah Shivaya.*

Om! Nahah Shivaya!

References

1. HISTORY AND PHILOSOPHY OF LINGĀYAT RELIGION. M. R. Sakhare, M.A., T.D. (Cantab). Karnataka University, Dharwad, India. 1978.

2. VEERASHAIVIM [VĪRAŚAIVISM] Fifth Edition. Soft cover print book ISBN: 9798772606612. Hard-cover print book ISBN: 9798761040151. Linga Raju amazon.com Modified February 2024.

3. IN SEARCH OF THE CRADLE OF CIVILIZATION. New Light on Ancient India. ISBN: 81-208-1626-9 (Cloth) ISBN: 81-208-2037-1 (Paper) Georg Feuerstein, Subhash Kak, and David Frawley. Motilal Banarsidass Publishers, Delhi, India. This Edition is reproduced from Quest Books 2001 Edition.

4. The Myth of The Aryan Invasion of India. ISBN: 81-85990-20-4 David Frawley (Vamadeva Shastri). Voice of India, 2/18 Ansari Road, New Delhi-110 002, India. Third Enlarged Edition: June 2005

5. Origin of the People of India and the Vedic Culture. Fifth Edition. Paperback print

book ISBN: 9781717850232 Linga Raju amazon.com Modified July 2024.

6. GODS, SAGES AND KINGS. ISBN: 1-878423-08-8 Vedic Secrets of Ancient Civilization, by David Frawley. Passage Press, Morison Publishing, P. O. Box 21713, Salt Lake City, Utah 84121, USA. 1991.

7. ṚGVEDA SAṀHITĀ according to the translation of H. H. Wilson, and Bhāṣya of Sāyaṇācārya, volumes I through IV. ISBN: 81-7110-139-5 (Vol I). ISBN: 81-7110-138-7 (set). Ravi Prakash Arya, K. L. Joshi. Primal Publications. Indica Books, D 40/18 Godowlia, Varanasi 221 001, India. 2002

8. The Rig Veda. Complete. ISBN: 978-1-60506-580-9. Translated by Ralph T. H, Griffith. Republished 2008 by Forgotten Books

9. THE BHAGAVAD GITA with Sanskrit Text. Translation by Swami Chidbhavananda. Published by The Secretary, Sri Ramakrishna Tapovanam, Tirupparaitturai, India. 1976

10. THE BHAGAVAD-GĪTĀ (The Song of God). ISBN: 81-208-1390-1. By Ramananda Prasad, Ph. D. Motilal Banarsidass Publishers

Private Limited, Delhi, India. Second Revised and Enlarged edition, Reprinted 1997

11. Śrī Śivayogi Śivācārya's Śrī Siddhāntaśikhāmaṇi with Śrī Maritoṇṭadārya's Tattvapradīpikā. ISBN: 81-86768-90-4 Dr. M. Sivakumara Swamy. Shaiva Bharati Shodha Pratisthan, Jangamwadi Math, Varanasi-221 001, India. 2007.

12. Gaṇaka Vachana Saṁpuṭa from taralabalu.org website. Sri Taraḷabāḷu Jagadguru Brihanmaṭh, Sirigere, Karnāṭaka, India.

13. A History of Indian Philosophy by Surendrantha Dasgupta, M. A., Ph. D. Volumes I through V. Cambridge at the University Press, London.

14. ŚŪNYASAṀPĀDANE. Volumes I through V. Published by Karnataka University, Dharwad, India.

15. Lingaadvaitism. Philosophy of the Lingayata Faith. Third Edition paperback soft cover print book ISBN: 9781521018637 Linga Raju. amazon.com website. Modified 2020.

16. Shaktivishishtadvaitadarshana (Kannada book) Dr. T. J. Siddhapparadhya, M.

A., Ph. D., Manasagangotri, Mysore University, Mysore. Shripanchacharya Press, Mysore. 1963.

17. KENOPANIṢAD by Swāmī Śarvānanda. ISBN: 81-7120-009-5. Sri Ramakrishna Math, Mylapore, Chennai 4, India. 2007.

18. Evolution of Veerashaiva Concepts. Fifth Edition in paperback print book ISBN: 9781520848709 Linga Raju amazon.com website. Updated 2020.

19. ŚVETĀŚVATAROPANIṢAD by Swāmi Tyāgīśānanda. ISBN: 81-7120-504-6. Sri Ramakrishna Math, Mylapore, Chennai 4, India. 2006.

20. HINDU SCRIPTURES. Essence of the Vedas, Upanishads, Bhagavad-Gītā, Purāṇas, Manu-smriti, Darshanas, Brahma-sūtras, Tantra, and Shivāgamas. Soft cover print book. ISBN: 9798534519938. Hard-cover print book. ISBN: 9798769243288. Linga Raju amazon.com website. Modified November 2021.

Printed in Dunstable, United Kingdom

66041226R00121